THE HISTORY

OF THE

RÜCKER AND PRIHODA FAMILIES

OF

BOHEMIA AND AMERICA

Earl F. Skelton, Ph.D., CG

HERITAGE BOOKS
2025

HERITAGE BOOKS

AN IMPRINT OF HERITAGE BOOKS, INC.

Books, CDs, and more—Worldwide

For our listing of thousands of titles see our website
at
www.HeritageBooks.com

Published 2025 by
HERITAGE BOOKS, INC.
Publishing Division
5810 Ruatan Street
Berwyn Heights, MD 20740

International Standard Book Number
Paperbound: 978-0-7884-1240-0

Acknowledgments

Thanks and appreciation are expressed to the many relatives who helped bring this family history together. First and foremost are my aunt and mother, Mary (née Rucker) Frotscher and Frances (née Rucker) Skelton, respectively. Had it not been for their help and continual encouragement, this work would not have come into being.

I am especially grateful to Aunt Mary for her depth of knowledge about our family. In spite of her now senior years, she has been able to recall names and events of many things that happened a long, long time ago. Throughout her life, Aunt Mary has maintained an active correspondence with many members of our extended family. These connections have been very helpful in the reconstruction of our genealogy. And many of the photographs which appear in this book come from Aunt Mary's collection of memorabilia.

The enthusiasm, countless suggestions, encouragement, and vigor of my mother, now in her ninetieth year, continue to amaze and impress me. Mom has been a constant source of motivation and inspiration to me, not just for this book, but throughout my life. As a proofreader and editor, there is none better. Mom can spot a dangling participle, a split infinitive, or a misspelled word at twenty paces — a talent which has remained undiminished over the years. Mom's enthusiasm and *joie de vivre* are highly contagious. Put her in a room full of people and before long, she'll have everyone's ear — and they'll all be smiling. Mom's help in creating this book has been vital.

Thanks are expressed also to my uncles, Eddie and Bep, who opened the family memory chest in Little Ferry and provided several of the older documents reproduced in the book. And gratitude is expressed to my first cousins, Rudy, Bob, and Bill, and my fourth cousin, Joseph, for the information they provided. I am also grateful to the members of the next generation for their help.

In short, this book — the history of our family — is a family production.

The editorial assistance of Mrs. Lisa M. Hightower-Chadwick of Camarillo, California is acknowledged with gratitude.

Earl Franklin Skelton

Table of Contents

List of Figures

Mary (née Rucker) Frotscher and Frances (née Rucker) Skelton on
10 May 1997 at the home of Mary Frotscher in Newburg, Pennsylvania

Foreword

At the beginning of the twentieth century, our parents, Matylda Prihoda and Adolf, later called "Otto," Rücker, then young adults, came to America. They left behind everything of the life they had known — their families, their friends, their homeland. Our mother and father met in America and began a family of their own, toiling daily and enduring the hardships that life put before them. Our parents spoke Czech at home and tried to maintain a connection to the rich heritage of the land of their birth, Bohemia. In time, five healthy children went from the Rucker household into the world — each to seek his or her own fortune.

Today, we approach the end of the twentieth century and the beginning of the fourth generation of descendants of Matylda and Adolf: Among their great-great-grandchildren are Joline Mariya Faujour (born 1991); Matthew Kilgore and Delora Kathline Faujour (both born 1993); Jessica Marie Kilgore and Ryan Samuel Hall (both born 1995); and William Franklin Heberlig, Dora Segal Skelton, and Patrick Hall (each born 1977). It is altogether fitting and proper that Earl Skelton, nephew of Mary, son of Frances, and grandson of Matylda and Adolf, should record, for generations to come, the history of our family.

We also thought it would be interesting for some of you of the future generations to read what life was like in the twentieth century. Perhaps some of you might decide to add what life is like in your generation for those who come after you.

Mary R. Frotscher

Mary (née Rucker) Frotscher

Frances R. Skelton

Frances (née Rucker) Skelton

Introduction

The objective of this work is to document the history of the Rücker and Prihoda families. The time period covered extends from the earliest known genealogical records of the families in Europe, *viz.*, the late seventeenth century to the present time, the end of the twentieth century. The earliest records are from the provinces of West and South Bohemia, in central Europe. Most of the immigrants entered America through the Port of New York and settled in the nearby communities of northern New Jersey. One branch began life in America in Chicago and later relocated to the midwestern city of Michigan City, Indiana.

Following the biographical background data on each of the known family members, a genealogical summary is given. These summaries are presented following the numbering system used in the *National Genealogical Society Quarterly*, also known as the *Modified Register System*. An effort has been made to cite all the sources for all the genealogical data.

Some members of the family in America adopted the German, rather than the Czech version of their name, *e.g.*, Rücker, rather than the Czech "Ricker" and Ignaz rather than the Czech "Hynek." Others anglicized their Czech names, *e.g.*, "Bedrich" to "Frederick". The version of a name used in this work will be that commonly used in the area under consideration, *e.g.*, "Prihodova" for women of the family in Bohemia, but "Prihoda" in America. The first time a name is encountered, the Czech version, if known, will be given in curly brackets, *e.g.*, Prague {Praha}, Moldau {Vltava}, and Rücker {Ricker}.

I. BOHEMIA AND THE CZECHS

The earliest known ancestors of the two families whose histories are documented in this work, the Rückers {*Rickers*} and the Přihodas, are found among the Czech people of central Europe. The Czechs embody two peoples, the Bohemians and the Moravians. Another ethnic group of the area are the Slovaks; they settled the land east of Moravia.

History

The history of the Czechs and Slovaks dates back to the fifth century, A.D., when Celts, followed by Germans, moved into the area. The sixth century brought the Slavonic tribes from the east, *viz.*, the area that is now Poland, just north of the Carpathian Mountains. Some of these tribes crossed the mountains into Moravia and Bohemia.[1] The largest was the Czech tribe, named for their leader. Four millennia later, the two groups were united in what was then the Great Moravian Empire. In the following century, the Slovaks were conquered by the Hungarians, while the Czechs began a five-hundred year period of political and military dominance in central Europe. The extent of this Bohemian Kingdom stretched, at one time, from the Adriatic Sea in the south, almost to the Baltic Sea in the north (see Fig. I-1). During this era, a large number of Germans immigrated into the region from the west and with this, began tensions between the Czechs and the Germans — tensions which have persisted well into the twentieth century.

An era of Czech self-expression came with the Hussite movement in the fifteenth century. Most historians consider the beginning of the Protestant Reformation as 1517, when Martin Luther (1483-1546) posted his "Ninety-five Theses on Indulgences" on the doors of the Palace Church in Wittenburg. But a century before that, the Czech preacher, Jan Hus (1369-1415), the son of a peasant from south Bohemia raised the same issues. He also challenged papal authority, and that led to his death.

A principal motivation for this reform movement was the decadence and corruption of the clergy. The wealth, privilege, and luxurious lifestyle of the nobles of the Catholic Church stood in stark contrast to the simple peasant lives of the fourteenth and fifteenth century. Jan Hus translated these disputes with the Church into broader social issues: rich against poor, German against Czech. By the time he began preaching in Prague at the Bethlehem Chapel, it had become the custom to preach sermons in the Czech vernacular, rather than the conventional Latin. His message was reaching the people. Hus also was dean

Fig. I-1. Kingdom of Bohemia and Its Extensions circa 1380.[2]

of philosophy faculty at Prague University and drew a great deal of inspiration from Jan Milič, a fourteenth century reformist, who sought to purify the Church and bring it closer to the people.[3]

In 1412, Hus was excommunicated by the Pope. For his safety, Hus then fled from Prague to Kozí Hrádek, a castle in Tábor. (See maps in Figs. I-1 and I-5.) From there, he continued his oppositionist teachings. Two years later, in 1414, Hus was summoned by Sigismund of Luxembourg, then the Holy Roman Emperor, and the ecclesiastical authorities of the Roman Catholic Church, to a council at Constance. Hus was asked to explain and defend his teachings and was given an imperial assurance of safe conduct and immunity. However, once in Constance, the "good" leaders of the Church had a change of heart. Hus was declared a heretic and rapidly dealt with in the manner fitting for those who disagreed with the Church: On 06 July 1415, Jan Hus was burned alive. Thus the Catholic Church rid itself of a trouble maker, but, at the same time, the first anti-Catholic martyr of the Reformation and a Czech national hero was created and the Hussite movement began.[4]

The Hussite religious reform movement developed into a national struggle for autonomy in political and ecclesiastical affairs. For over two centuries, the Czechs were able to maintain political self-rule. This was expressed by the Bohemian estates (an assembly of nobles, clergy, and townspeople representing the major social groups in the Bohemian Kingdom) and the Czech Reformed Church.[5]

In 1526, the Bohemian estates voluntarily accepted a Hapsburg ruler as a monarch. A century later, conflict developed between the Czechs and the Hapsburgs which eventually led to war. This armed confrontation ended in 1620 (the same year that the *Mayflower* landed at Plymouth Rock) with the Battle of White Mountain {Bilá Hora}, fought just outside Prague {Praha}. There were about twenty thousand men representing the Bohemian estates and slightly more, about twenty-five thousand, mercenaries led by a Catholic Spanish-Flemish nobleman. The battle lasted less than an hour and the professional soldiers quickly scattered the poorly organized Czechs. The consequences of defeat were severe: (1) the Czech leadership was either killed or sent into exile; (2) the reformed Czech religion was eliminated; (3) the Czech language went into decline; (4) the remnants of the Bohemian Kingdom were abolished; and (5) all

Czech lands were incorporated into Austria. The Czechs had lost their self-rule and were reduced to an oppressed nation.[6]

During the nineteenth century, the status of the Czech people improved. One reason for this was that in the first part of the century, František Palacký, a Moravian historian, was appointed by the ruling Austrians, as the official historiographer of the Kingdom of Bohemia. Serving in this role, he wrote a monumental book, in both Czech and German, entitled *History of the Czech Nation in Bohemia and Moravia.* This had a very positive effect on the development of the Czech people. Contemporary Czechs no longer looked upon themselves as simple peasants, but were filled with pride, based upon the achievements of their ancestors. They again began to believe in the future.[7] This improved self-image of a people, accompanied by a vigorous industrialization, transformed the Czechs from a peasant people into a differentiated society, including industrial workers, a middle class, and intellectuals.

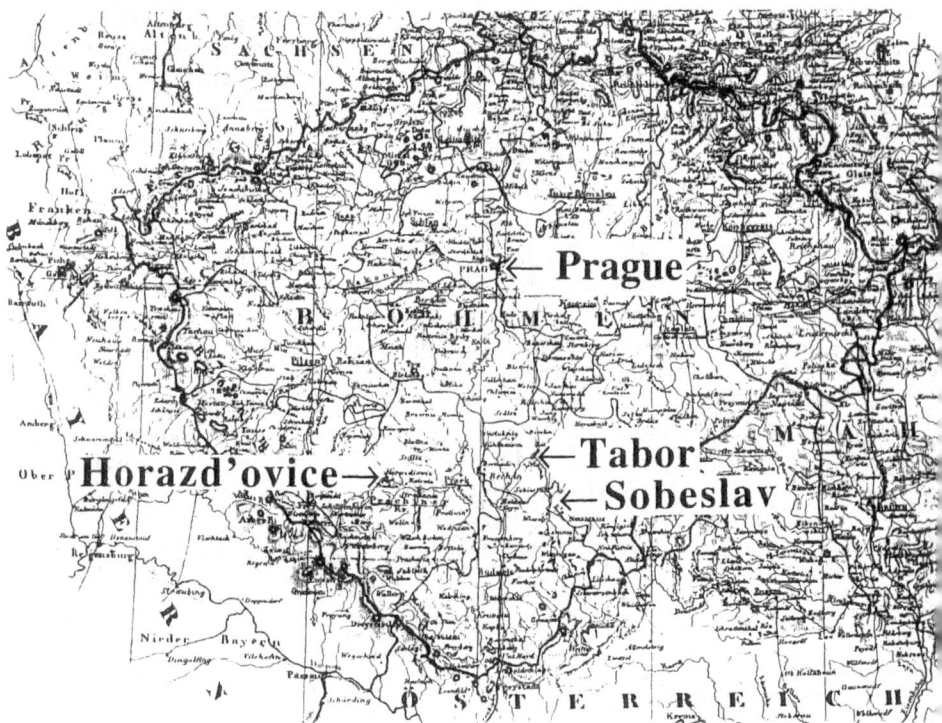

Fig. I-2.   A map of Bohemia, circa 1844.[8]   The locations of the capital of Prague and the towns of Tabor, Horažd'ovice and Soběslav have been identified.

Fig. I-3. Czech Republic circa 1997 including Bohemia and Moravia.

By the middle of the nineteenth century, the Czechs were making political demands on the ruling Austrian parliament. Among these were the restoration of an autonomous Bohemian Kingdom. However, fearing they might lose their privileged position, the German element living in Bohemia vigorously opposed such a state. It was on the eve of World War I that the Czech leader, Tomáš Masaryk, proposed the idea of a reunification of the Czechs and Slovaks into a single political entity: Czechoslovakia. This came to pass in 1918, at the end of World War I.

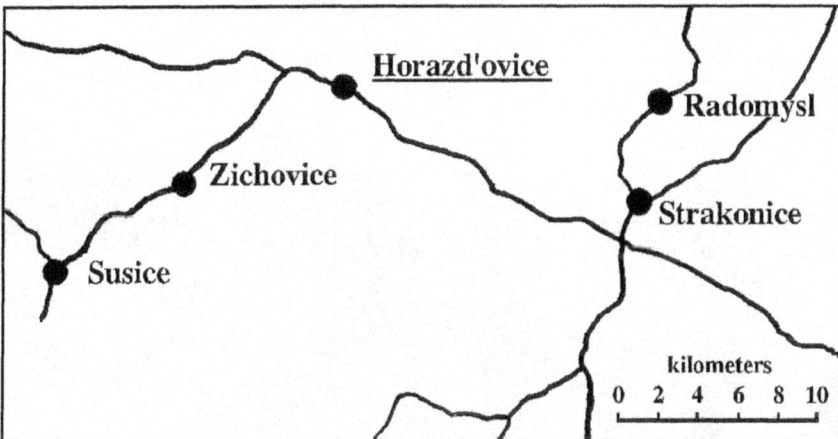

Fig. I-4. Enlargement of the area around Horažd'ovice, showing its location relative to several nearby villages.

The Republic of Czechoslovakia lasted for twenty years. On 28 September 1938, in an effort to appease Hitler's Third Reich, Britain and France ceded the western part of Czechoslovakia, known as the Sudetenland, to Germany. Six months later, in March 1939, the Nazis occupied all of Bohemia and Moravia — Czechoslovakia ceased to exist.

In 1945, at the end of World War II, Czechoslovakia was reconstituted as an independent nation. The pluralistic political system of Czechoslovakia lasted only three years. In February 1948, the democratically elected president, Beneš, was overthrown in a coup by the Communist Party of Czechoslovakia. Twenty years later, in the spring of 1968, Alexander Dubček attempted to introduce a more democratic form of socialism into Czechoslovakia. This was crushed in the spring of 1968 by troops from the five Warsaw Pact countries.[9]

In the 1980's, with the disintegration of the Soviet empire and the remaking of the Soviet state, democratization was no longer hindered in Czechoslovakia (nor in Poland or Hungary). The Czech Republic of today consists of two regions: Bohemia, to the west, and Moravia, to the east. Bohemia is subdivided into five political divisions {kraje}: North Bohemia {Severočeský}, South Bohemia {Jihočeský}, East Bohemia {Východočeský}, West Bohemia {Zàpadočeský}, and Central Bohemia {Středočeský}. Moravia consists of two central political divisions: North Moravia {Severomoravský} and South Moravia {Jihomoravský}. The Republic of Slovakia is divided into three parts: East Slovakia {Východoslovenský}, Central Slovakia {Stredoslovenský}, and West Slovakia {Západoslovenský}.

Fig. 1-5. Enlargement of the area around Soběslav and Tabor,
showing the location of the town of Velká Chýška,
about 38 km (24 mi.) northeast of Soběslav.

The Czech people have a rich heritage in the arts. One demonstration of
this is an exhibition recently held in North Carolina.[10] For seven months,
beginning in September 1996, a large and varied selection of Czech art was
borrowed from the Czech National Museum in Prague and exhibited in Winston-
Salem, North Carolina.

Geography

The land of all but a small portion of Bohemia drains into the North Sea by
way of the Moldau {Vltava} and Elbe {Labe} Rivers. The hills and low
mountains that encircle Bohemia are part of the north-central European uplands
that extend from southern Belgium, through the central lands of Germany, and

into Moravia. These uplands are known geologically as Hercynian Massif. They are distinct from the Alps and Carpathian Mountains to the south and east, respectively.

Bohemia's mountainous areas differ greatly in population. The northern regions of the Erzgebirge {Ore} and Sudeten Mountains are densely populated, whereas the less hospitable Český les Mountains and Šumava Mountains to the south are among the most sparsely populated areas in Bohemia.

Most of the streams in Bohemia flow from all directions through the Bohemian Basin toward Prague. The central lands of the Bohemian Basin are lower in elevation, but their features vary widely. There are small lakes in the central southern region and in the Moldau Basin north of Prague. Some of the western grain lands are gently rolling, where other places have deep gorges cut by streams and rivers, such as the Moldau.

<u>Location of the Rücker and Prihoda Families</u>

The earliest known location of the Rücker family is in the town of Horažd'ovice; the earliest known location of the Prihoda family is in the town of Soběslav. Both Horažd'ovice and Soběslav are located in the southern portion of Bohemia. Two enlargements of a modern map of southern Bohemia are reproduced in Figures I-4 and I-5. The first (Fig. I-4) is centered on Horažd'ovice and includes the nearby cities of Sušice and Strakonice. The second (Fig. I-5) is centered on the town of Soběslav and includes the adjacent villages of Nedvědice and Debrnik, and the town of Velká Chýška. Records of the family have been found in each of these locations.

The town of Soběslav was founded by Prince Soběslav II. It was in possession of the Rožmberks in the thirteenth century and elevated to the status of a town in 1390. Still standing in the town today is a view tower preserved from a castle built in the latter half of the fourteenth century. Remnants of the town fortification and middle-class houses of the Renaissance period are also preserved, as is a Gothic church from the end of the fourteenth century. Today, Soběslav is home to the District Museum of the Tábor Region and among its holdings are collections of natural history in the Rožmberk House and exhibitions of ethnography and architecture.[11]

II. THE RÜCKER FAMILY

First and Second Generations

Ignaz {Hynek or Ignác} Rücker {Ricker} -I is the oldest known member of the Rücker family. The earliest record uncovered for him is that of his marriage on 04 February 1822 in the town of Horažd'ovice in West Bohemia to Josefa Veselá.[12] Ignaz -I died in Horažd'ovice on 20 March 1855 and was buried two days later in the Cemetery of St. John {Jan}. At death, his age was reported as either 79 or 83, making his year of birth either 1776 or 1772, respectively. The parish records for Josefa Veselá indicate that she was born in 1793, the daughter of Jan Veselý, the master saddle maker of Strakonice, and his wife, Josefa Růžičková.

Ignaz Rücker -I and Josefa Veselá were parents to five children, all born in Horažd'ovice. Their second child was Ignaz Rücker -II, born on 16 February 1826. Thirty-five years later, on 05 February 1861, also in Horažd'ovice, Ignaz -II married Marie Schütz {Süc}, the daughter of Jan Schütz, a master bookbinder in Horažd'ovice, and Rosalie Koželoužek.

Ignaz -II and Marie were parents to eight children; all but the second were born in Horažd'ovice. Their first child, Ignaz Rücker -III was born on the last day of 1860. Technically, he was "illegal," as the marriage of his parents took place thirty-six days after his birth. However his father, Ignaz Rücker -II, claimed responsibility for his son, Ignaz Rücker -III.

The second child of this marriage was Tomáž Jindřich Rücker, born 10 October 1862 in the town of Bohumilice, located in South Bohemia. According to the birth records, during this period Ignaz-II, the master butcher from Horažd'ovice, was a tenant of the pup or inn at Bohumilice.

The third and seventh children of Ignaz -II and Marie were Karel, born 28 January 1866, and Adolf, born a decade later, on 23 October 1876. Karel and Adolf are the only members of this family known to have immigrated to America — Karel in about 1885 and Adolf in the spring of 1903.

The Rücker family has maintained a presence in the town of Horažd'ovice for many generations, down to the present time. Many made their livelihoods there as members of the working middle class. The professions found among the family include: store keeper [Ignaz Rücker -I], master butcher [Ignaz Rücker -II], master bookbinder [Jan Schütz], and master saddle maker [Jan Veselý].

Third Generation

Tomáž Jindřich Rücker (1862-1945)

On leap day, 29 February, in the year 1892, Tomáž Jindřich Rücker married Albina Protivová and on 19 June of the following year they had a son, Ladislav Josef Rücker. Unfortunately, Ladislav did not live beyond that first day of his life. Four days later his mother also passed away. Four months after that, on 03 October 1892, Tomáž married for a second time. His new bride was Josefa Pometlová, who was born on 10 June 1874.[13] Tomáž and Josefa were parents to four children: Marie, Ladislav, Václav, and Ferdinand.[14]

Charles Rücker (1866-1947)

The first member of the family known to immigrate to America was Karel Rücker, an older son of Ignaz Rücker-II and Marie (née Schütz) Rücker. In America, Karel's forename was anglicized to "Charles," but he also has been found in the records as Kaarel, Karel, and Carl. According to the U.S. census records, Charles was born in Bohemia in 1866; from cemetery records, his date of birth is calculated to be 18 January 1866. Both records are in reasonable agreement with the date of his birth as recorded in the Horažd'ovice Parish register: 28 January 1866.

According to the 1900 census, Charles arrived in America in 1886;[15] according to the 1910 census, he arrived 1885;[16] and according to the 1920 census, in 1887.[17] Family lore has it that Charles arrived in New York City circa 1885 and worked for the next five or six years as a butcher in nearby Hoboken, New Jersey.

On 25 November 1891, at 269 Clinton Avenue in West Hoboken, New Jersey, Charles Rücker married Barbara Kukal. Barbara was the daughter of Joseph Kukal and Maria (née Perinova) Kukal. Although both Charles and Barbara were born in Bohemia, they probably met in West Hoboken. On their marriage certificate, Charles' address is given as "No. 352 Spring Street, West Hoboken, N.J." and Barbara's as "No. 358 Spring Street, West Hoboken, N.J." This was the first (and only) marriage for each of them.

Bergen County is the most northeastern county in the State of New Jersey. It is bounded on the north by New York State and on the east by the Hudson River. On 18 September 1894, the area known as "Little Ferry" was formally separated from the Township of Lodi and incorporated as an independent borough.[18] Its name is derived from the ferry that once served as a means of crossing the Hackensack River. In the late nineteenth century and later, the manufacture and sale of clay bricks was a principal business of the community. Today the area is dotted with water filled pits, marking spots where clay has been extracted.

On 23 October 1894, five weeks after the Borough of Little Ferry was incorporated, Charles and Barbara Rücker paid $1750 for Lots 3, 4, and 5, on the north side of Washington Avenue, adjacent to the intersection with Marshall Avenue.[19] [It is interesting to note that Washington Avenue is said to have been named for an event that took place during the Revolutionary War. In the fall of 1776, the fledgling American Continental Army was in retreat from the British, who then occupied the City of New York. On November twentieth of that year, a detachment of the army became separated from the main force. This detached unit crossed the Hackensack River at the rope drawn ferry, near the modern town of Little Ferry. They then marched several miles north to the town of Hackensack, where they rejoined the Continental Army and General Washington. Their march was via a street known today as *Washington Avenue*.[20]] It was on these three lots on Washington Avenue that Charles founded the family slaughter house and butchery. The following February, he, Barbara, and their then five month old daughter, Mary, relocated from West Hoboken to 138 Washington Avenue, Little Ferry.[21]

According to the 1920 census record, Charles became a naturalized citizen of the United States in 1897.[22] From property and other extant records, it is clear that he and his family had relocated from Hudson County to Bergen County in 1895, yet no evidence of his naturalization in Bergen County has been located.[23] [A search in Hudson County also has been unsuccessful.]

The family butchery and grocery store operated successfully until 1960. At one time four butchers were working in the business. The slaughtering of the livestock, cows, pigs, and calves, was done on site, the animals being purchased from local farms. Charles was a very successful businessman. During the period from 1895 to 1909, he purchased twelve additional pieces of property. Several of these included dwellings of significance.[24]

Recorded with Charles and Barbara in the 1900 census,[25] as renters in their home, are William and Antonia Valek (both born in Bohemia) and their seven month old son, Charles.[26] In 1901, Charles and "Welham Welek" borrowed $1000 from Henry S. Little, David St. John, and Sheffield Phelps, each of Teaneck, New Jersey, to purchase property adjacent to the Hackensack River.[27] In the baptismal records of the Church of the Immaculate Conception, Barbara Rucker is listed as the sponsor for Mary Weleck, daughter of William Weleck and Antonia "Gugal."[28] Assuming that "Valek," "Welek," and "Weleck" each refer to the same surname, and that the surname "Gugal" was actually "Kukal", it is inferred that Barbara and Antonia were sisters, thus making Charles Rücker and William Weleck brothers-in-law. William's occupation is reported in the census as "butcher." According to Mary (née Rucker) Frotscher, a niece of Charles Rücker, William Weleck owned and operated another butcher shop, then located on Main Street in Little Ferry.[29]

Charles Rücker and Barbara (née Kukal) Rücker had six children, four of whom survived to adulthood, *viz.*, Mary, Carolina, also known as "Carrie," William Charles, and Charles William. (Two sons died early.) As reported below, Mary Rucker was murdered in 1912. Barbara (née Kukal) Rücker died two years later, from a cerebral hemorrhage, and also was interred in the family plot.

Charles never remarried but, according to family lore, he became entangled with several women, one of whom later sued him for breach of promise. In anticipation of a judgment against him, on 30 December 1926, Charles transferred ownership of many of his properties to his older son, William.[30] Again according to family lore, after the lawsuit was settled, William would not return the properties, arguing that his father was no longer "responsible."

A heavy cigar smoker, Charles died from lung cancer on 05 April 1947 and was buried in the family grave site three days later. His entire estate, except for ten dollars, was left to his younger son, Charles William Rucker:[31] Here are the details of his will: (1) To Carrie Vaclavicek (née Carolina Rucker) the sum of $10. "The reason I am not giving her a larger share in my estate is that I have given her large sums of money during my lifetime." (2) "The reason why I am not making any provision in this my Last Will and Testament for my son, William C. Rucker, is that he has received from me very large sums of money during my lifetime, in fact, a great deal more than would otherwise be his share in my estate." (3) "Everything else, real and personal, goes to Charles Rucker, Jr." [Charles signed his will on 27 April 1935 and he signed as "Charles Rücker" — with the umlaut.]

On Monday, 07 April 1947, the following obituary was published:[32]

Charles Rucker, Sr., 81, of 138 Washington Avenue, Little Ferry, a resident of Little Ferry for the past 56 years, died Saturday morning at Hackensack Hospital.

He was born in Czechoslovakia and his family there had a record of 300 years as butchers. He was a butcher all his life and established one of Little Ferry's first butcher shops 57 years ago. It is now operated by his son, Charles, Jr.

Funeral services will be conducted by the Rev. Frederick V. MacPeck pastor of the Little Ferry Congregational Church tomorrow at 2 P.M. at the Trinka Funeral Home, 198 Main Street, Little Ferry. Burial will follow at New York Cemetery, Hackensack.

Four organizations will conduct services tonight at the funeral home: Susquehanna Tribe 252, Improved Order of Red Men will conduct services at 8 P.M., Workman's Sick and Death Benefit at 8:15, Little Ferry Rotary Club at 8:30, and Lodge Bratri Od Sazavy at 8:45.

He is survived by a daughter, Mrs. Charles Vaclavicek of Maywood and two sons, Dr. William C. Rucker of Hackensack and Charles Rucker, Jr. of Little Ferry.

Adolf Rücker (1876-1938)

Adolf Rücker was a younger brother of Charles. According to the 1910 census, Adolf was born in 1877 in Bohemia, immigrated to America in 1903, and listed his trade as butcher.[33] These data are consistent with Horažd'ovice Parish records giving his date of birth as 23 October 1876 and his father's trade as master butcher. In September of 1918, when he completed his World War I draft registration card, Adolf reported his date of birth as "Oct. 23rd, 1876. (See Fig. II-3.)

During his crossing of the Atlantic, Adolf was issued an orange card by the Red Star Line. On the reverse side of this card, it is explained in eight different languages (none of which is English), that the card needed to be completed very carefully and presented to the immigration authorities upon arrival in America. A copy of Adolf's card is reproduced in Figure II-1.

It is interesting to note that on the obverse side of the card shown above, and in response to the question: *"I will go to... "*, Adolf wrote, "my Brüder Charles Rücker, Little Ferry, New York."[34] The word "York" is scratched out in pencil and written next to it, also in pencil, and in a different handwriting, is the word "Jersey."

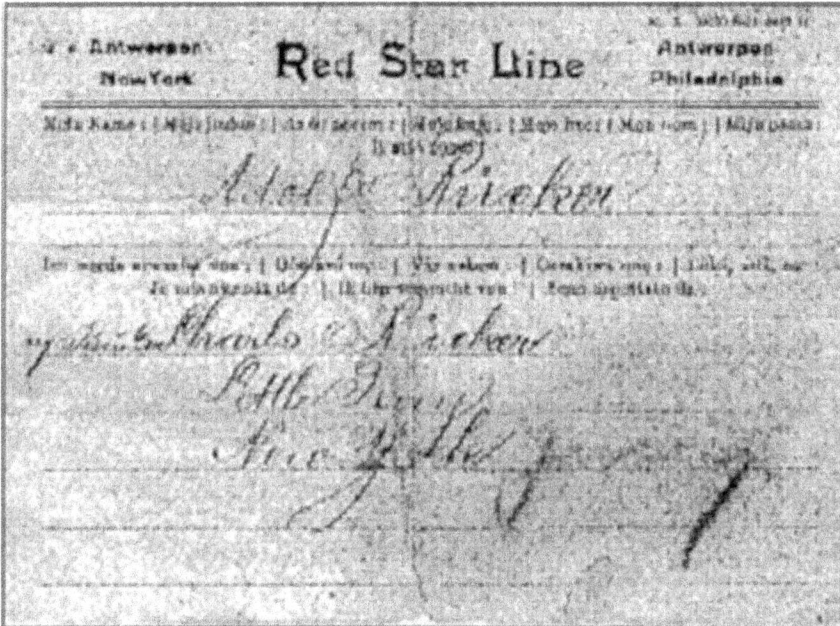

Fig. II-1. Immigration Card of Adolf Rücker filled out in 1903.

Using that card and his approximate year of arrival as a guide, Adolf Rücker's entry records into the United States have been located.[35] He departed from Antwerp, Belgium on Saturday, 18 April 1903 and arrived at the Port of New York ten days later, on Tuesday, 28 April 1903. He crossed the Atlantic Ocean aboard the *S.S. Vaderland*, a ship of the Red Star Line. He reported that he had $10 in his possession, that his passage had been paid by his brother, and that he was going to join his brother, "Karel Rücker" in "Little Ferry, New York, NY." In the manifest of alien passengers, Adolf listed his occupation as a butcher and appears to have been traveling alone.

Presumably in late April or early May 1903, Adolf arrived at his brother's butcher shop on Washington Avenue in Little Ferry, New Jersey and went to work. A year later, in Manhattan, New York City, New York, Adolf married Matylda Prihodova. The following information has been extracted from their Czech marriage certificate:[36]

Groom:	*Adolf Rücker*
Place of Birth:	*Horažd'ovice v. Čechách*
Bride:	*Matylda Prihodova*
Place of Birth:	*Velké Chyšky v. Čechách*
Date:	*"tretiho července devatenácistého*
	čtortého" [= 03 July 1904]
Witnesses:	*Charles Rücker*
	Bohnue Vevera

Adolf Rücker became a naturalized citizen of the United States. His Declaration of Intention to become a citizen, or so-called "first papers," was filed in the federal court in Hackensack on 31 March 1910.[37] In 1916, he filed his "final papers" and on 16 June 1916, he was declared by the court to be a citizen of the United States of America. His Certificate of Naturalization was issued a week later, on 23 June. It has been preserved in the family archives;[38] a copy is reproduced in Fig. II-4.

On the upper portion of Adolf's Certificate of Naturalization, he is described as 39 years of age; 5 feet, 8 inches tall; white in color; fair in complexion; with blue eyes and light brown hair; and no distinguishing marks. The information in the middle part describes his family, by name and age, and their residence in Little Ferry, New Jersey. In the middle of the certificate is his signature. It is noted that the umlaut still appears above the "u." Near the lower central part of the document, it states that "...previous to his naturalization [Adolf Rücker] was a subject of Franz Joseph, Emperor of Austria and King of Prussia..."

Prior to 1922, the law specified that when a husband acquired citizenship, his wife automatically became naturalized too. Thus, on 16 June 1916, Matylda (née Prihodova) Rücker also became a citizen of the United States. All their children, of course, were citizens by birth.

Adolf was a member of The American Sokol of Little Ferry. The word *sokol* means falcon and the organization was dedicated to the concepts of liberty, equality, brotherhood, and mutual cooperation. Objectives of the organization were for its members to keep physically and morally fit to serve their country and to "...speak the truth, love the truth, and live by the truth."[39]

Fig. II-2. Members of the American Sokol of Little Ferry, New Jersey.
Adolf Rucker (with hat) is standing at the extreme right, in the second row.

It is believed that the above photograph was taken circa 1914, when there were forty-eight states in the Union. (Arizona, the forty-eighth state, was admitted on 14 February 1912.) The American flag, on the left in the photo, contains forty-five stars, which means it was appropriate during the period from 04 January 1896, when Utah was admitted as the forty-fifth state, and 16 November 1907, when Oklahoma entered as the forty-sixth. The flag on the right in the photo is believed to be white on top and red on the bottom, which is the national flag of Poland. However, Adolf's daughter, Frances, recalls very clearly her mother's admonitions that *they were NOT Polish*. It is believed to be the Bohemian flag.

During the *Great War* — World War I, there were three separate draft registrations required by congressional conscription acts. The first was on 05 June 1917 and included all men between the ages of 21 and 31; the second was in June and August 1918 and included all men who had become 21 since the first draft; and the third and final draft was on 12 September 1918 and required all men in the age groups of 18 - 21 and 31 - 45 to register. Adolf Rucker was included in the last group. Below is a copy of the obverse side of his draft registration card.[40]

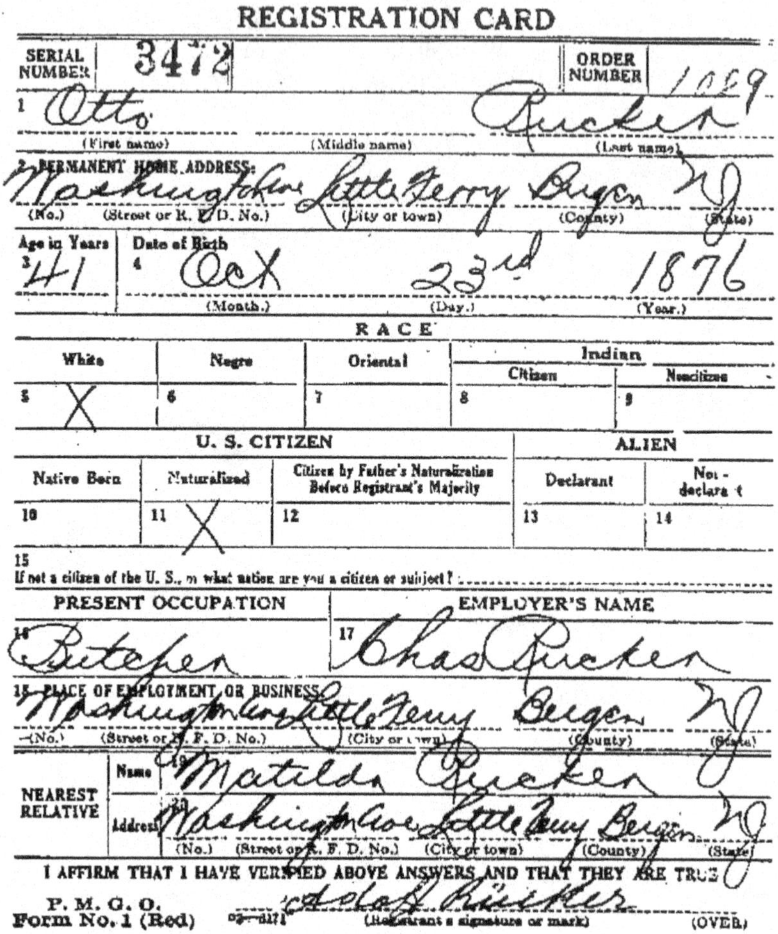

REGISTRATION CARD

SERIAL NUMBER 3472 ORDER NUMBER 1029

1 Otto Rucker
(First name) (Middle name) (Last name)

2 PERMANENT HOME ADDRESS: Washington Ave Little Ferry Bergen NJ
(No.) (Street or R. F. D. No.) (City or town) (County) (State)

Age in Years 3 41 Date of Birth 4 Oct 23rd 1876
(Month.) (Day.) (Year.)

RACE

White	Negro	Oriental	Indian Citizen	Indian Noncitizen
5 X	6	7	8	9

U. S. CITIZEN Native Born	U. S. CITIZEN Naturalized	U. S. CITIZEN Citizen by Father's Naturalization Before Registrant's Majority	ALIEN Declarant	ALIEN Non-declarant
10	11 X	12	13	14

15 If not a citizen of the U. S., of what nation are you a citizen or subject?

PRESENT OCCUPATION 16 Butcher EMPLOYER'S NAME 17 Chas Rucker

18 PLACE OF EMPLOYMENT OR BUSINESS: Washington Ave Little Ferry Bergen NJ
(No.) (Street or R. F. D. No.) (City or town) (County) (State)

NEAREST RELATIVE Name 19 Matilda Rucker
Address 20 Washington Ave Little Ferry Bergen NJ
(No.) (Street or R. F. D. No.) (City or town) (County) (State)

I AFFIRM THAT I HAVE VERIFIED ABOVE ANSWERS AND THAT THEY ARE TRUE

P. M. G. O. Form No. 1 (Red) Adolf Rücker (Registrant's signature or mark) (OVER)

Fig. II-3. Obverse side of the World War I draft registration card of Adolf Rücker.

On the reverse side of the card, Adolf is described as of medium height and build, with blue eyes and sandy color hair. It is curious that the name of the registrant is given as "Otto Rucker," yet the registrants' signature at the bottom is clearly "Adolf Rücker."

On Thursday, 02 June 1938, at the family home in Little Ferry, Adolf died. The cause of death was lobar pneumonia. His remains were interred in the Rucker family plot six days later. In the cemetery records, he also is recorded as "Otto Rucker," not Adolf.[41] The information probably was supplied to the cemetery officials by his wife. As is reported in Part IV of this work, "The Prihoda Family History," Matylda never liked the forename "Adolf." In the 1920 census,[42] on his World War I draft registration,[43] and in the records of the New York Cemetery, it was "Otto." In the 1910 census[44] and on his naturalization records,[45] it was "Adolf."[46]]

Biographical sketches and the descendants of Adolf Rucker and Matylda (née Prihodova) Rucker are presented under "The Prihoda Family History."

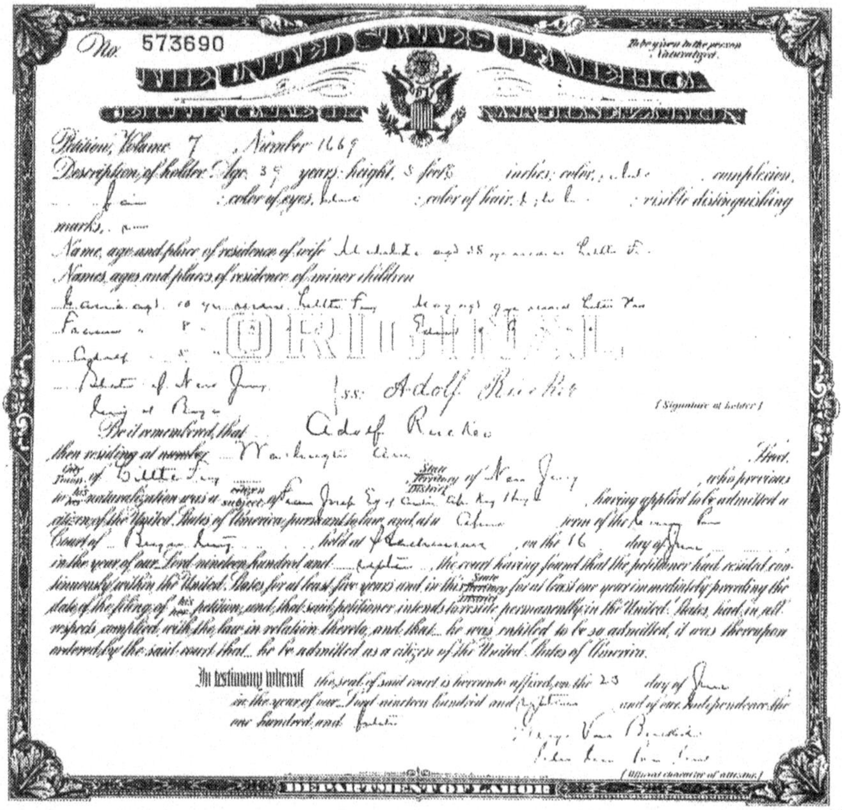

No. 573690

To be given to the person Naturalized.

THE UNITED STATES OF AMERICA

CERTIFICATE OF NATURALIZATION

Petition, Volume 7, Number 1169

Description of holder: Age, 39 years; height, 5 feet, inches; color, white; complexion, fair; color of eyes, blue; color of hair, ; visible distinguishing marks, none

Name, age and place of residence of wife

Names, ages and places of residence of minor children

ORIGINAL

Adolf Rücker (Signature of holder)

Be it remembered, that Adolf Rücker then residing at number Washington Ave Street, City of , State of New Jersey, who previous to his naturalization was a subject of Franz Joseph Emp of Austria , having applied to be admitted a citizen of the United States of America pursuant to law, and at a term of the Court of , held at , on the 16 day of June in the year of our Lord nineteen hundred and sixteen the court having found that the petitioner had resided continuously within the United States for at least five years and in this State for at least one year immediately preceding the date of the filing of his petition, and that said petitioner intends to reside permanently in the United States, had in all respects complied with the law in relation thereto, and that he was entitled to be so admitted, it was thereupon ordered by the said court that he be admitted as a citizen of the United States of America.

In testimony whereof the seal of said court is hereunto affixed on the 23 day of June in the year of our Lord nineteen hundred and sixteen and of our Independence the one hundred and fortieth.

(Official character of attestor.)

DEPARTMENT OF LABOR

Fig. II-4. Naturalization Certificate of Adolf Rücker, No. 573690 dated 23 June 1916.

Fourth Generation

Children of Tomáž Rücker and Josefa Pometlová

Tomáž and Josefa were parents to four children: Marie, Ladislav, Václav, and Ferdinand.[47] Marie married Jan Roučka and they had a store in which they sold animal hides. They had no children. Ladislav never married and was a local office holder. Václav and Ferdinand both married, Václav to Růžena Smucarová and Ferdinand to Anna Hošková. They also both followed in the family tradition of buchery. Ferdinand and Anna had no children, but Václav and Růžena had two sons: Václav and Jaroslav.

Descendants of Tomáž Rücker Presently Living in the Czech Republic[48]

Tomáž Rücker had only two grandchildren, the aforementioned Rücker sons Václav and Jaroslav. Both married and produced great-grandchildren: Václav had a son and a daughter, Václav (-III), born in 1954 and Marie, born in 1957. Václav (-III) is single and is a salesman in a food store. Marie, a saleswoman in a textile store, married Zdeněk Kadlec. Marie and Zdeněk had a daughter in 1986: Marie Kadlecová.

Jaroslav had only one child, a son, born in 1964 and also named Jaroslav. Jaroslav (Jr.) is a plumber and married. He and his wife, Iveta (née Jánská), have two children, a daughter named Nela Rückerová, born in 1988, and a son named Aleš Rücker, born in 1990.

Murder of Mary Rucker (1894 - 1912)

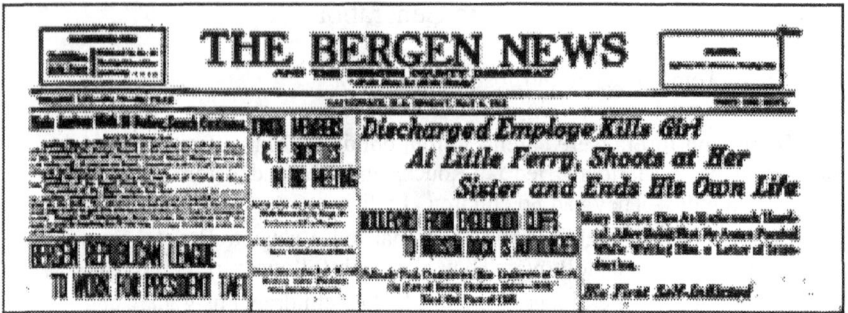

Fig. II-5. Upper portion of the front page of *The Bergen News* on 06 May 1912.

Fig. II-6. Carolina (Carrie) and Mary Rücker in the late 1890's.

One month after the *Titanic* sank, Mary Rücker, the oldest child of Charles and Barbara (née Kugal) Rücker, was murdered. This happened at about a quarter after one on Sunday afternoon, 05 May 1912. Mary was only seventeen years old; she would have celebrated her eighteenth birthday in September The details of this heinous crime were reported in three newspapers: *The New York Times, The Bergen News,* and *The Hackensack Republican.* The following account is based on these news articles.[49]

In 1908, one of the butchers working in Charles' shop was a German immigrant named Anton Parchal, a young man in his early thirties. Sometime around 1910, Parchal returned to Germany for a visit. When he returned, he resumed work in the Rücker butchery — for a while. In December of 1911, he was discharged for reasons that Charles Rücker would not disclose. Parchal left without a word of complaint and was not seen by the family for the next six months.

On Saturday evening, 04 May 1912, a dance was held at the Sokol Hall in Little Ferry. The two Rücker daughters, Mary and her younger sister, Carrie, attended the dance. Anton Parchal was there too. Early the next morning, Parchal went to the Rücker store to request a letter of reference. He said he wanted this so that he might obtain another job. Barbara, the girls' mother, told him to come back at one o'clock in the afternoon.

At about one, Parchal entered the family portion of the store through a rear door. There he found Mary sitting at a desk. She was writing the letter of recommendation that he had requested earlier. Carrie was sitting beside her, Barbara was in the front of the store, and Charles was resting in bed upstairs. As Mary was about to give the letter to Parchal, she must have seen the 38-caliber revolver in his hand — she leapt to her feet and started to run. Parchal fired instantly, the bullet striking her on the left side. She staggered forward, in an apparent effort to reach her mother in front of the building, and then fell, unconscious to the floor in the doorway.

Parchal then turned the gun on himself and shot himself harmlessly through his left breast. Next Carrie ran screaming from the room. Parchal followed her and fired as she was going through the street door. Fortunately, at that moment, she stumbled and fell. This probably saved her life. The bullet missed her and went crashing through the store window and into the house across the street.[50] Possibly believing that both girls were dead, Parchal then shot himself again, this time through the heart. He died instantly.

Mary, still unconscious, was rushed in a hurriedly summoned ambulance to the Hackensack Hospital. She died within twenty minutes of her arrival, never regaining consciousness.

There are conflicting speculations as to the motive for the murder. According to the neighbors, Parchal had attempted, on several occasions, to display his affection for Mary. She was not interested. Apparently he had been drinking heavily at the Sokol Hall the night before and was very jealous when Mary danced with several young men that she had known since early childhood. As reported in the *Times*, "It was said by some that Parchal was insanely jealous of Miss Rucker, who was one of the most popular girls in Little Ferry..." However, according to Mary's father, this "rejected suitor" reason was nonsense. Here are the words of Charles Rucker: "This was no love matter at all, and it is cruel even to suggest such a thing. It is said this fiend saw a young man accompany Mary and her sister home from a reception last night, and became insanely jealous, but I do not believe that is so. It's a mighty good thing for him he killed himself. I believe he intended to kill me and all my family. To think he murdered my little girl as she was writing out a few good words about him so that he could get work!" The letter that Mary was about to give to Anton Parchal just before he murdered her read as follows:

> *Little Ferry, May 6*
>
> *This will introduce Anton Parchal who worked four years in my slaughter house.*
>
> *Charles Rucker*

If Charles Rücker's argument is correct and Parchal wanted to murder the entire family, then why did he turn the gun on himself so soon? There was no immediate threat to him. If the true object of his rage had been Charles Rücker, then why did he not ask to see him when he entered the shop and shoot him first? And Barbara Rucker was in the area, but escaped unharmed.

It is curious that there appears to be no record of the death of Anton Parchal in the New Jersey Bureau of Vital Statistics.[51] And what became of his remains is unknown. Family lore speculates that he was buried in an unmarked grave in the "Potter's Field" portion of the New York Cemetery.

It was in the wake of this tragic event that Mary's father purchased the Rücker Family Plot in the New York Cemetery, now called the Maple Grove Park Cemetery, on Hudson Street in Hackensack, New Jersey.[52] A report on the Rucker Family Plot is given in the following section.

Carolina (née Rucker) Vaclavicek (1896-1967)

Fig. II-7. Carolina, or "Carrie," Rücker circa 1913.
The document in her left hand is believed to be a diploma.

At 9:30 in the evening of Tuesday, 26 March 1918 in Little Ferry, Carolina, better known to the family as "Carrie," married Charles Vaclavicek. Charles was born circa 1895 in Union Hill, New Jersey, the son of Thomas Vaclavicek and Francis [sic] Hereman. At the time of his marriage, Charles reported his residence as New Durham in Bergen County, New Jersey and his occupation as soldier. He later worked in the butcher shop of his father-in-law. He was often called by his initials, "CV".

Carrie and Charles lived at 67E Hunter Avenue in Maywood and had only one child: Charles Vaclavicek, Junior. Carrie died in 25 October 1967 and three days later was interred in the George Washington Memorial Park Cemetery.

On 26 October 1967, the following Death Notice appeared in *The Record:*[53]

VACLAVICEK — Carrie (nee Rucker) on October 25, 1967 of 67 E Hunter Avenue, Maywood. Beloved wife of Charles and devoted mother of Charles W. Funeral services at Trinka's, 439 Maywood Avenue, Maywood on Saturday at 10:30 A.M. Interment George Washington Memorial Park. Family will receive their friends 7-9 Thursday and 3-5 and 7-9 on Friday.

William Charles Rucker (1903-1970)

The older son, William Charles Rucker, graduated from Brown University in Providence, Rhode Island. In 1931, he was a member of the graduating class of Tufts Medical School, Tufts University in Medford, Massachusetts.[54] He did post-graduate work at Massachusetts General Hospital in Boston and The George Washington University in Washington, DC. For many years, Dr. Rucker practiced as the company physician of Bendix Corporation in Teterboro, New Jersey. He also maintained a private practice, was senior attending physician of orthopedics at the Hackensack Hospital (now called the Hackensack Medical Center), and a member of the Bergen County American Medical Association and of the New Jersey Association of Industrial Physicians and Surgeons.

"Doc" Rucker, as he was called by the family, married late in life — his bride also was a member of the medical profession: Dr. Vendela Olson, an anesthesiologist at the Hackensack Hospital. Their home, at 308 Union Street, was located at the corner of Clay and Union Streets in Hackensack.[55] Doc and Vendela had no children; much of their spare time was spent traveling and sailing on their forty-two foot yacht.

Doc was also known as Commodore Rucker, a title conferred upon him by the Yacht Club of Englewood, New Jersey. He was a past commander of the Yacht Club and a member of the Rotary Club, the Explorers' Club, and the United States and Saddle River Power Squadrons. A licensed ham radio operator, Doc was also a member of the Rotarians of Amateur Radio and of the Medical Amateur Radio Council, Ltd. He produced films for local organizations and belonged to the Photographic Society of America and the Amateur Cinema League.[56]

It was during a trip to the homeland of his parents in Europe that William Charles Rucker passed away. This happened during a stopover in Hannover, Germany. The cause of death was an embolism. He had one in his leg and another in his chest that lodged in his right ventricle.[57] He died on 27 July 1970 and his remains were returned to the United States by air. To comply with various governmental regulations, his body was transported in three coffins. Because Vendela had a fear of flying, she returned by boat and the funeral was delayed. The remains of William Charles Rucker are interred in the George Washington Memorial Park Cemetery in Paramus, New Jersey.

Fig. II-8. William Charles Rucker, in his early twenties.

The details of the will of Doc Rucker are interesting.[58] His last will and testament is dated 15 July 1970 — only twelve days before he died. Here is a synopsis: Item 1 directs that all his just debts be paid; Item 2 leaves his entire estate to his wife, Vendela O. Rucker; Item 3 makes Vendela the executrix of the estate (no bond required); Item 4 specifies the disposition of his estate in the event that Vendela predeceases him or they die at the same time. There are extensive details, but the effect is to distribute the estate of William Rucker among the relatives of his wife.

Dr. Vendela (née Olsen) Rucker received her medical degree from the University of Minnesota and later an M.S. in hospital administration from Columbia University. She was director of medical services at St. Luke's Hospital in New York and was the first president of the Bergen and Passaic Lung Association. In 1982, she was honored by the association, being elected to their Seventy-fifth Anniversary Hall of Fame. Vendela died on 05 March 1984 and also is interred in the George Washington Memorial Park Cemetery in Paramus, New Jersey.[59]

Charles William Rucker (1908-1980)

Charles William Rucker was born on Friday, 31 July 1908 in Little Ferry. Following the death of his father, Charles, called "Butch" by friends and family, took over the family butcher business on Washington Avenue in Little Ferry. He too seems to have been successful. He later relocated to the west and at one time owned and operated the Imperial Motel in Orange County, California.

Charles married Elizabeth (or Betty) Obeda and they had only one child, a son named Carlton born in the late 1930's in New Jersey. Charles died at the age of 73 in Florida in 1980. At the time of his death, his residence was 1537 Owen Drive, Clearwater, Florida and his occupation was reported as "Proprietor; Meat Store."[60]

[At the time of this writing, Betty (née Obeda) Rucker and her son, Carlton W. Rucker, continue to live in Hackensack.[61] Neither have chosen to communicate with the author regarding this work.]

Genealogical Summary:
Descendants of Ignaz Rücker and Josefa Veselá

1. **Ignaz[1] {Hynek} Rücker {Ricker}** was born circa 1772-1776; died 20 March 1855; buried 22 March 1855 in the cemetery of St. John {Jan} in the town of Horažd'ovice in southern Bohemia, in what was then Austrian Empire. Ignaz was a storekeeper in the town of Horažd'ovice No. 84. His age at the time of death was reported to be "79 or 83."[62,63]

On 04 February 1822 in Horažd'ovice, Ignaz Rücker married **Josefa Veselá**.[64] Josefa was born circa 1793 in Strakonice, the daughter of Jan Veselý and his wife, Josefa Růžičková. Josefa died 23 July 1863 at Horažd'ovice No. 84 and was buried on 25 July in the cemetery of St. John by D. Thomás Býček. She also was Catholic and her last testament was given on 23 July 1863 by D. Josef Cikán.[65]

Ignaz and Josefa had five children; all were born in Horažd'ovice:[66]

	2	i.	Karolina Joanna Rücker[2], born 03 November 1824.
+	3	ii.	Ignaz {Hynek} Rücker, born 16 February 1826; died 02 June 1893 in Horažd'ovice.
	4	iii.	Antonin Thomas Rücker, born 17 September 1827.
	5	iv.	Jindřich Quirin Rücker, born 23 March 1829. The following note is made in the parish register by the vicar: "Died like the soldier."
	6	v.	Marie Anna Eva Rücker, born 24 December 1831; died probably 10 December 1832.

3. **Ignaz[2] {Hynek} Rücker** (Ignaz[1]) was born on 16 February 1826 in Horažd'ovice.[67] The following information is recorded in the parish record about his birth: "On 16 February 1826 from Horažd'ovice No. 81 was born Ignác /de Loyola/Simon Ricker; Catholic, male, from the legal bed. The father: Ignác Ricker, the citizen and the store-keeper from here. The mother: Josefa, the daughter of deceased Jan Veselý, the citizen and the master saddler from Strakonice, and the mother Josefa, born Růžičková. The godfathers: - Tomáš Sedmihráský, the master cobbler from Stebnice /?/; - Anna, the wife of Kosák, the miller from Stebnice /?/. Baptized on 17.2.1826 [= 17 February 1826] Wenceslaus Pýcha, Capellator. The midwife: Marie Boháčová." Ignaz died on 02 June 1893 at House No. 104 in Horažd'ovice.[68]

On 05 February 1861 in Horažd'ovice, Ignaz Rücker married **Marie Schütz {Süc}**.[69] The following information is given with their marriage record: "On 5 February 1861 were from Horažd'ovice - the town No. 84 married by D. Josef Cikán, Caplan: the bridegroom: Hynek [= Ignaz] Rücker, the citizen and the master butcher in Horažd'ovice - the town No. 84, the legal son of deceased Hynek Rücker, sometime the citizen and the store-keeper in Horažd'ovice - the town No. 84, and still alive the mother Josefa, born Veselá from Strakonice No. 46, the caunty Horažd'ovice. He is Catholic, single, 34 years old. The bride: [= Schütz, in German], the legal daughter of still alive Jan Süc, the citizen and master book-binder in Horažd'ovice - the town No. 61, and also still alive mother Rosalie, born Koželoušková, from Sušice No. 64, the caunty Horažd'ovice. She is Catholic, single, 23 years old. The witnesses: Josef Schwetz, the scribe; Ignaz Kaučka, the master tanner. The marriage bands of matrimony were on 23 January, 2nd and 3rd February in the local church. The permit for the matrimony of not adult daughter gave Johann Schütz, the father."

Marie Schütz was born on 02 September 1837.[70] The following information is given in the parish record of her birth: "On 2nd September 1837 was born in Horažd'ovice - the suburb No. 110 Marie Schütz, Catholic, female, from the legal bed. Baptized on 3rd September Joannes Drbal, Cappellanus. The father: Jan Schütz, the citizen and the master book-binder. The mother: Rosalie, the daughter of deceased Václav Koželoužek, the citizen and master tailor from Sušice, the mother Magdalena, born Ledecká from Sušice No. 64. The godfathers: Marie and Josef _____ [the surname impossible to read], master black-smith in _____ [difficult to read]." [No death record has been located for Marie Schütz. This could be because she died after 1896 and the records are still in the city hall or she may have died in a parish other than Horažd'ovice.]

Ignaz Rücker and Marie Schütz were parents to eight children; all, except the second, were born in Horažd'ovice:[71]

> 7   i.   Ignaz {Hynek} Rücker[3] born 31 December 1860; married 08 February 1887 in Horažd'ovice, Vojtěška, the daughter of František Čapek, the butcher in Horažd'ovice. [In the Czech records it is noted that Ignaz {Hynek} was not legal because he was born a month before his parents were married. However, his father Ignaz {Hynek} Rücker (b. 1826) confirmed that he was the father.][72]

> +   8   ii.   Tomáž Jindřich Rücker born 19 October 1862 at Bohumilice No. 50 in South Bohemia; died 19 June 1945.

+   9   iii.   Charles Rücker, born 18 January 1866; died 05 April 1947 at the Hackensack Hospital, Hackensack, Bergen County, New Jersey.

     10   iv.   Františka Rücker, born 02 April 1868. [She had an illegal daughter born on 21 April 1889.][73]

     11   v.   Joseph Rücker, born 13 February 1872.

     12   vi.   Marie Rücker, born 03 March 1874.

+   13   vii.   Adolf Rücker, born 23 October 1876; died 02 June 1938 at the family home at 135 Washington Avenue, Little Ferry, Bergen County, New Jersey; buried 08 June 1938 in the New York Cemetery (now called the Maple Grove Park Cemetery) in Hackensack, New Jersey.

     14   viii.   Antonie Klára Rücker, born 23 February 1880.

8. **Tomáš Jindřich[3] Rücker** (Ignatz[2], Ignatz[1]) born 19 October 1862 at Bohumilice No. 50, near Vimperk in South Bohemia. (At this time in 1862, Ignaz Rücker, the father of Tomáš, was a tenant of the pub or inn at Bohumilice.);[74] died 19 June 1945;[75] married (1) 29 February 1892 in Horažd'ovice, **Albina Protivová**; died 23 June 1893 in Horažd'ovice; married (2) 03 October 1893 in Horažd'ovice, **Josefa Pometlová**;[76] born 10 June 1874; died 20 October 1937.[77] Tomáš and Albina had only one child, a son, who was born and died on the same day in Horažd'ovice:[78]

     15   i.   Ladislav[4] Josef Rücker, born 19 June 1893; died 19 June 1893.

Tomáš and Josefa were parents to four children, all born in Horažd'ovice:[79]

     16   ii.   Marie Rücker, born 27 January 1900; died 06 September 1986; married Jan Roučka. They had no children and ran a store selling animal hides.

     17   iii.   Ladislav Rücker, born 27 August 1901; died 25 August 1974. Never married and worked as a local official (office holder).

+   18   iv.   Václav Rücker, born 09 August 1902; died 09 March 1967; married 08 December 1928, Růžena Šmucarová.

     19   v.   Ferdinand Rücker, born 14 May 1906; died 08 October 1982; married Anna Hošková, born 09 February 1909; died 22

January 1991. Ferdinand was a butcher and he and Anna had no children.

9. **Charles**[3] **Rücker** (Ignatz[2], Ignatz[1]) born 28 January 1866 in Horažd'ovice;[80] died 05 April 1947 at the Hackensack Hospital, Hackensack, Bergen County, New Jersey; buried 08 April 1947 in the New York Cemetery (now called the Maple Grove Park Cemetery) in Hackensack;[81] married 25 November 1891 at 269 Clinton Avenue, West Hoboken, Hudson County, New Jersey, **Barbara Kukal**, born October 1871 (or 1870) in Bohemia,[82] the daughter of Joseph Kukal and Maria Perinova, his wife;[83] died 21 August 1914 at the Rücker family home on Washington Avenue, Little Ferry, Bergen County, New Jersey; buried 23 August 1914 in the New York Cemetery.[84] Charles and Barbara were parents to six children, four of whom survived to adulthood.[85]

20	i.	Mary Rücker[4], born 07 September 1894 at 424 Spring Street in West Hoboken;[86] murdered 05 May 1912 at her home on Washington Avenue in Little Ferry; buried 08 May 1912 in the New York Cemetery.[87]
21	ii.	Carolina (aka "Carrie") Rücker, born 17 December 1896 in Little Ferry; died on 25 October 1967 in the Hackensack Hospital and buried 28 October 1967 in the George Washington Memorial Park Cemetery, Paramus, Bergen County;[88,89] married 26 March 1918 in Little Ferry, Charles Vaclavicek, born 1895 in Union Hill, New Jersey, the son of Thomas Vaclavicek and Francis [*sic*] Hereman.[90] Carolina and Charles had only one child, a son, Charles Vaclavicek, Junior.[91]
22	iii.	unnamed son who died early
23	iv.	unnamed son who died early
24	v.	William Charles Rucker, born 28 October 1903[92] in Little Ferry; christened 03 July 1904 in the Church of the Immaculate Conception at 49 Vreeland Avenue, Hackensack; died at 11:35 PM on 27 July 1970 at a hotel located at Marienstraße 78 in Hannover, Germany;[93,] buried in the George Washington Memorial Park Cemetery;[94,95,96] married 28 April 1945 in Hackensack, Dr. Vendela Xvelyn Olson, born 14 October 1905 in Minneapolis, Minnesota, the daughter of John D. Olson and Ida Eklund;[97] died 05 March 1984 in Hackensack; buried in the George Washington Memorial Park Cemetery, Paramus.[98,99,100] William and Vendela had no children.

25   vi.   Charles William Rucker, born 31 July 1908 in Little Ferry; christened 02 August 1908 in the Church of the Immaculate Conception; died 21 August 1980 at the Morton F. Plant Hospital, Clearwater, Pinellas County, Florida; buried in the George Washington Memorial Park Cemetery;[101] married at St. Mary's Church on Hudson Street, Hackensack, Elizabeth (aka, Betty) Obeda. Charles and Elizabeth had only one child, a son, Carlton W. Rucker, born about 1938 in the Hackensack Hospital.[102]

13. **Adolf[3] Rücker** (Ignatz[2], Ignatz[1]) born 23 October 1876 in Horažd'ovice;[103,104] died 02 June 1938 at the family home at 135 Washington Avenue, Little Ferry, Bergen County, New Jersey; buried 08 June 1938 in the New York Cemetery (now called the Maple Grove Cemetery) in Hackensack;[105] married 03 July 1904 in the Borough of Manhattan in New York City, **Matylda Prihodova**.[106,107] Matylda was born 15 March 1875 in Velká Chýška, in southern Bohemia, the daughter of Karel Prihoda and Jana Moravec;[108] died 09 March 1947 at 153 Fairmont Avenue, Maywood, New Jersey; buried 12 March 1947 in the New York Cemetery.[109]

On Saturday, 18 April 1903, Adolf departed from Antwerp, Belgium bound for the United States of America. He arrived at the Port of New York ten days later: Tuesday, 28 April 1903. Adolf crossed the Atlantic Ocean aboard the *S.S. Vaderland*, a ship of the Red Star Line.[110]

Seven years later, on 31 March 1910, he filed his "first papers" to become a U.S. citizen at the federal court in Hackensack.[111] And six years after that, on 16 June 1916, Adolf was declared by the court to be a citizen of the United States of America. His Certificate of Naturalization was issued on 23 June 1916.[112] Two years later, during World War I and in compliance with the congressional conscription acts, on 12 September 1918 Adolf registered with the local draft board.[113]

Adolf and Matylda were parents to six children, five of whom survived to adulthood.[114]

*   26   i.   Carolina ("Carrie") Rücker[4], born 17 January 1906 at 52 Garden Street, Little Ferry; christened 29 April 1906 at the Church of the Immaculate Conception in Hackensack;[115] died 27 July 1962 in Ridgewood, New Jersey; buried 30 July 1962 in the George Washington Memorial Park Cemetery, Paramus, New Jersey;[116,117] married 24 July 1927 at the Church of the Immaculate Conception, Rudolph Komarek,[118] born 05 October 1903 in Bohemia; died 20 February 1987 in Louisville, Kentucky; buried 23 February 1987 in George Washington Memorial Park Cemetery.[119]

*   27   ii.   Mary Rucker, born 21 January 1907 at 135 Washington Avenue, Little Ferry; christened 02 August 1908 at the Church of the Immaculate Conception in Hackensack;[120] married 09 July 1929 in Newport, Kentucky, William Franklin Frotscher,[121] born 11 October 1903 in Bellevue, Campbell County, Kentucky, the son of Herman C. Frotscher and Elizabeth Barteswelt;[122,123] died 27 January 1990 in Chambersburg Hospital, Chambersburg, Pennsylvania; remains cremated 28 January 1990 by the Smithsburg Crematory, Smithsburg, Washington County, Maryland.[124]

*   28   iii.   Frances Rucker, born 04 April 1908 at 135 Washington Avenue, Little Ferry;[125] christened 02 August 1908 at the Church of the Immaculate Conception in Hackensack;[126] married 02 August 1931 at the Evangelical Congregational Church in Little Ferry, Floyd Skelton,[127] born 03 September 1904 in Dayton, Campbell County, Kentucky, the son of Isaac Franklin Skelton and Augusta Dieterle;[128] died 18 October 1982 at home, 215 Shippensburg Road, Shippensburg, Hopewell Township, Pennsylvania; remains cremated 20 October 1982 by East Harrisburg Crematory, Harrisburg, Dauphin County, Pennsylvania.[129]

29   iv.   Edward Rucker, born 01 August 1909 at 135 Washington Avenue, Little Ferry; served in the U.S. Army during World War II.[130]

30   v.   Adolph Rucker, born 22 December 1910 at 135 Washington Avenue, Little Ferry; served in the U.S. Army during World War II.[131]

31   vi.   Matylda Rucker born 15 March 1917 at 135 Washington Avenue, Little Ferry; died 05 April 1917; buried 09 April 1917 in the New York Cemetery (now called Maple Grove Cemetery), Hackensack.[132]

18. **Václav[4] Rücker** (Tomáš Jindřich[3] Ignatz[2], Ignatz[1]) born 09 August 1902 in Horažd'ovice; died 09 March 1967; married 08 December 1928, **Ružena Šmucarová**, born 17 March 1902; died 05 January 1954. Václav was a butcher and he and Ružena were parents to two children:[133]

+   32   i.   Václav Rücker[5], born 22 January 1930; died 17 September 1991; married Marie Nová.

+   33   ii.   Jaroslav Rücker, born 21 August 1933; married Marie Suchanová.

32. **Václav^5 Rücker** (Václav^4, Tomáš Jindřich^3 Ignatz^2, Ignatz^1) born 22 January 1930; died 17 September 1991; married Marie Nová, born 09 September 1927. Václav was a salesman in a store specializing in leather merchandise. He and Marie were parents to two children, a son and a daughter:[134]

34   i.   Václav Rücker^6, born 28 July 1954. Václav is a salesman in a food store and is single.

35   ii.   Marie Rücker, born 08 May 1957; married Zdeněk Kadlec, born 02 April 1955. Marie is a saleswoman in a store dealing with textiles. She and Zdeněk have a daughter, Marie Kadlecová, born 13 February 1986.

33. **Jaroslav^5 Rücker** (Václav^4, Tomáš Jindřich^3 Ignatz^2, Ignatz^1) born 21 August 1933; married Marie Suchanová, born 24 February 1939; died 07 July 1989. Following in the family tradition, Jaroslav was a butcher. He and Marie had only one child.

36   i.   Jaroslav Rücker^6, born 14 November 1964; married Iveta Jánská, born 01 October 1966. Jaroslav is a plumber and he and Iveta have two children, a daughter, Nela Rücková, born 25 May 1988, and a son, Aleš Rücker, born 10 March 1990.[135]

---

* Descendants of these people are developed under Genealogical Summary: Descendants of Jan Příhoda and Žofie Zimová which begins on page 161.

III. THE RÜCKER CEMETERY PLOT

The Maple Grove Park Cemetery, originally called the New York Cemetery, was created in 1851 by members of the True Reformed Dutch Church of the City of New York. At the time, this church was located on King Street in New York City. Its first trustees were Seba Brinkerhoff, Cornelius Bogert, Ralph Terhune, and Ralph I. Westervelt, surnames that continue to be familiar in Bergen County, New Jersey. The opening paragraph in the original publication, describing the New York Cemetery, is interesting:[136]

> This Cemetery is located near the village of Hackensack, N.J., fronting on the main Turnpike road [now Hudson Street] from Hoboken to said village, ten miles distant from the City of New York. Lines of Stages pass the Cemetery regularly several times daily. It is situated on an eminence, commanding a beautiful and extensive view of the Hackensack River, and the country for miles on the east bank of the Hackensack, spread with its rich fields, forests and hills — the beautiful and quiet village of Hackensack, with its white dwellings and numerous spires, and of the country adjoining, with its mountain and valley scenery — no spot in the State embraces a greater variety of landscape or more picturesque view.

Location of the Cemetery

Known today as the Maple Grove Park Cemetery, its address is 535 Hudson Street, Hackensack, New Jersey 07601. The location of the cemetery, about a mile north of U.S. Route 46 and about a mile west of the Hackensack River, is shown in Figure IV-11.

As discussed earlier, on Sunday, 05 May 1912, Mary Rücker, the elder daughter of Charles Rücker and Barbara (née Kukal) Rücker, was murdered by Anton Parchal, a one time employee of her father. It was this tragic event that caused Charles to purchase the Rücker Family Plot in what was then the New York Cemetery. Charles bought twenty-four single grave sites, each eight feet by three feet. This is a square of land, twenty-four feet on a side, containing an area of 576 square feet. Its location in the cemetery is shown in Figure III-1.

On Monday, 06 May 1912, Charles Rücker paid the New York Cemetery Association $144.00 for the twenty-four graves in Lot 35 of Section E.[137] The current (1998) price for a single grave in Maple Grove Park Cemetery is $925; so today, these twenty-four graves would cost in excess of eleven thousand dollars. A snapshot of the right portion of the family plot, as it was on 07 May 1996 is shown in Figure III-2; the left portion is shown in Figure III-6.

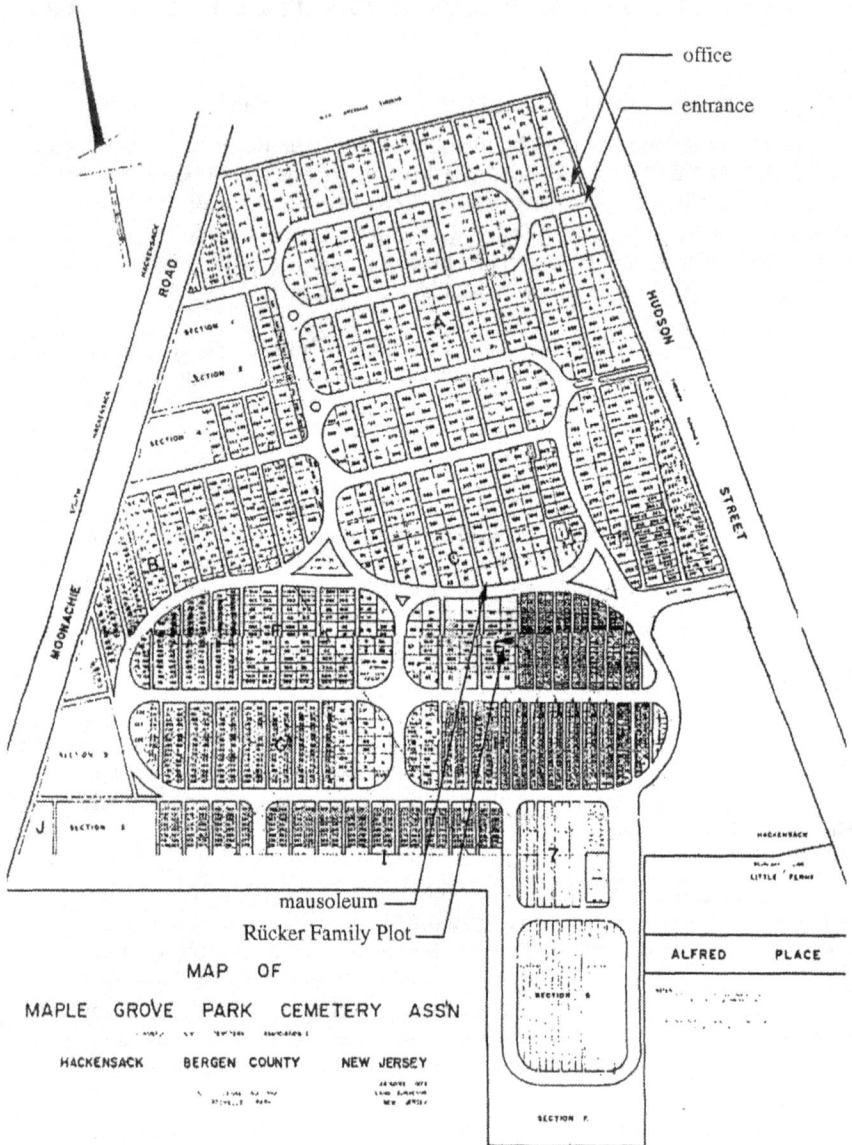

Fig. III-1. Location of the Rücker Family Plot in the
Maple Grove Park Cemetery at 535 Hudson Street, Hackensack, New Jersey
(Used with permission of the Maple Grove Park Cemetery Association.)

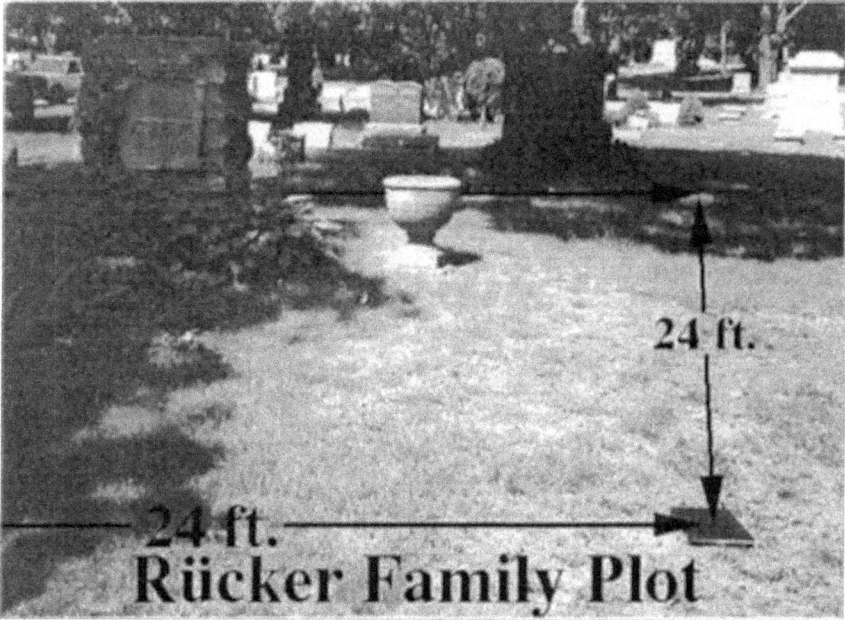

Fig. III-2. Right portion of the Rücker Family Plot in the Maple Grove Park Cemetery, Hackensack, NJ. The book in foreground at the right marks the front right corner of the plot; the white stone in the upper right marks the back right corner.

17	18	19	20	21	22	23	24
9	10	11	12	13	14	15	16
1	2	3	4	5	6	7	8

Path

Rucker, Charles
No.s 35 & 35N Sec.E
Size 24 X 24

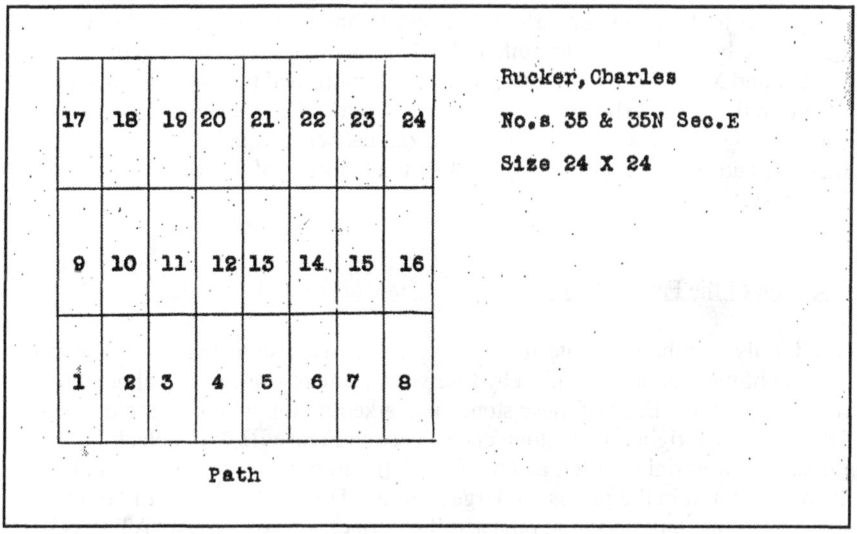

Fig. III-3. Obverse side of the Maple Grove Park Cemetery record for the plot purchased by Charles Rücker in 1912.

Int.No.	Name	Gr.No.	Int.No.	Name	Gr.No.
		1			13
	Joseph Kukel	2			14
	Frank Kukel	3			15
9360	Anna Agler 1/18/52	4			16
7615	Frank Alger	5			17
		6		Mary Rucker	17
		7		Barbara Rucker	18
		8	6092	Charles Rucker, Sr.	19
		9		Adolph Rucker	20
		10		Matylda Rucker	21
		11			22
		12	8884	Matylda Rucker	23
					24

Fig. III-4. Reverse side of the Maple Grove Park Cemetery record for the plot
purchased by Charles Rücker in 1912.

The cemetery records for this family plot, as copied in the Maple Grove
Park Cemetery office on 07 June 1996, are shown in Figures III-3 and III-4. The
two names in italics and underlined, corresponding to graves 20 and 21 in Figure
III-6, have been added by the author. Each of the four living children of Adolf
Rucker and Matylda (née Prihoda) Rucker has confirmed that their parents are
buried in this plot. Why their names are not included in the cemetery card
shown above is not known. (This omission has been brought to the attention of
Mrs. Barbara Kirby, President of the Board of Trustees of the Maple Grove Park
Cemetery.)

Location of the Family Graves

Ten family members are interred in this plot; six have stone markers. The four
corners of the plot are identified by four white, square stones, each about ten
inches on a side. Each of these stones is marked on top with the single letter,
"R." The back right corner stone can be seen in Figure III-2; the black book
marks the front right corner, and the front left corner stone is identified in Figure
III-6. Centered in the plot is the largest stone. This is at the head of Graves 4
and 5. On the upper portion, on a scroll of stone, are two words: "AT REST"
and below that, the family surname is written: "RUCKER." This stone is
pictured in Figure III-5.

Fig. III-5. Rucker Family Stone, centered in the grave plot.

The two graves immediately in front of the "Rucker Family Stone," Graves 4 and 5, contain the remains of Frank and Anna Agler. Anna is née Kukal, the sister of Barbara (née Kukal) Rucker, and hence the sister-in-law of Charles Rucker, the plot owner. Frank Kukal was her husband. There are four stones associated with these two graves, one at each of the heads and one at each of the feet. The head stones contain the following inscriptions: "ANNA AGLER 1869 — 1952" and "FRANK AGLER 1856 — 1935," respectively. The foot stones say "WIFE" and "HUSBAND," respectively. It is noted that on the grave card shown in Figure III-4, Anna's surname is spelt "Agler" and Frank's is "Alger."

On both stones, the spelling is "Agler." The surname on the card for Frank is probably a typographical error. The fact that the foot stones identify Anna and Frank as "Wife" and "Husband," respectively, rather than "Mother" and "Father," suggests that the couple may not have had children.

Fig. III-6. Left portion of the Rucker Family Plot. The front left "R" marker stone is in the foreground. The location of the occupied graves, as listed on the above cemetery record, are identified by number. The mausoleum identified on the cemetery map (Fig. III-1) is identified in the upper right corner of the photograph.

Graves 2 and 3, located immediately to the left of Graves 4 and 5, have only two head stones. These read "FATHER" and "FRANK," respectively. Both graves are outlined by a cement border, but the one for Frank (#3) has sunken into the ground. These graves contain the remains of Joseph Kukal and Frank Kukal, respectively. They were the father-in-law and brother-in-law, respectively, of Charles Rucker.

In the back left corner of the plot are graves 17 and 18. They contain the remains of Mary Rücker, the murder victim in 1912, and Barbara (née Kukal) Rücker, her mother, the daughter and wife, respectively, of Charles Rucker. The stone for Mary is inscribed, "MARY RUCKER 1894-1912," and that for Barbara says, "BARBARA RUCKER 1872-1914."

Buried adjacent to Barbara Rücker in Grave 19 is her husband, Charles Rucker, the original purchaser of the plot. Ironically, there is no marker for his grave. Buried adjacent to Charles, in Graves 20 and 21, are Adolf Rucker and Matylda (née Prihoda) Rucker, younger brother and sister-in-law, respectively, of Charles Rucker. There are no markers for these graves either.

The seventh body interred in this plot is that of Matylda Rucker, a sixth child born to Adolf and Matylda in 1917. Baby Matylda lived for only twenty-five days. The cemetery records show her to have been interred in Grave 23. However, family lore says that upon the death of her father in 1938, her remains were transferred and interred at the feet of her father in Grave 20.

<u>Cemetery Records</u>

The current custodian for the cemetery is Mrs. Barbara Kirby, President of the Board of Trustees of the Maple Grove Park Cemetery. Mrs. Kirby was very helpful in providing the following information for each member of the family interred in the cemetery to the author. The records are listed by grave number in the Rucker plot. (These records were not photocopied; Mrs. Kirby read the information from the cemetery record book to the author.)

<u>Grave 2:</u> Joseph Kukal; last residence - Little Ferry, New Jersey; age at death - 89 years; interred - 02 March 1917; cause of death - cerebral hemorrhage; father of Barbara Rucker.

<u>Grave 3:</u> Frank Kukal; last residence - Hackensack, New Jersey; age at death - 20 years, 4 days; interred 20 October 1918; cause of death - pneumonia.

<u>Grave 4:</u> Anna Algar [*sic.*; the correct spelling of the surname is believed to be "Agler."]; born in Czechoslovakia; last residence - Hackensack, New Jersey; age at death - 82 years; interred 18 January 1952; cause of death - multiple scleroses; undertaker - Riccardo and Sons Funeral Home.

<u>Grave 5:</u> Frank Agler; last residence - Hackensack, New Jersey; age at death - 79 years, 10 months, 2 days; interred 18 December 1935; cause of death - lobar pneumonia.

<u>Grave 17:</u> Mary Rucker; last residence - Little Ferry, New Jersey; age at death - 17 years, 7 months, 27 days; interred - 02 May 1912 [*sic,* the correct date of death is 05 May 1912]; cause of death - gun shot wound; daughter of Charles and Barbara Rucker.

Grave 18: Barbara Rucker; last residence - Little Ferry, New Jersey; age at death - 43 years; interred - 23 August 1914; cause of death - cerebral hemorrhage.

Grave 19: Charles Rucker; last residence - Little Ferry, New Jersey; age at death - 81 years, 2 months, 17 days; died - 05 April 1947; interred - 08 April 1947; cause of death - cancer of the lungs; undertaker - Trinka Funeral Home.

Grave 20: Otto[138] Rucker; born in Bohemia; last residence - Little Ferry, New Jersey; age at death - 61 years; died - 02 June 1938; interred - 08 June 1938; cause of death - lobar pneumonia; widow - Matylda Rucker.

Grave 21: Matylda Rucker; last residence - Little Ferry, New Jersey; age at death - 71 years, 11 months, 22 days; died - 09 March 1947; interred - 12 March 1947; cause of death - chronic myocarditis; undertaker - Wokal Funeral Home.

Grave 23: Matylda Rucker; last residence - Little Ferry, New Jersey; age at death - 25 days; interred - 09 April 1917; cause of death - pneumonia; child of Otto and Matylda Rucker.

IV. THE PRIHODA FAMILY

First Four Generations

The earliest known event for this family occurred in 1692, the same year in which twenty people were executed by the "good" citizens of Salem, Massachusetts for the "crime" of witchcraft. On 21 January 1692, in the small central European town of Soběslav, located in Jižní Čechy Province in southern Bohemia, a much happier event took place: Jan Příhoda married Žofie Zimová.[139,140] That wedding marked the beginning of what is known of this Příhoda family. For the next century and a half, the family remained near the village and manor of Soběslav in southern Bohemia.

From 1701 to 1713, Jan and Žofie became parents to six children. Their youngest child was Andreas {Ondřej} Příhoda who was baptized in Soběslav on 16 November 1713. The godfather named at the baptism was Kašpar Zelenka; the witnesses were Josef Nestler-[?] and Mařena Vorlová.[141]

A quarter century later, on 10 November 1739, Andreas Příhoda took a bride: Anna Duchwaldová, the daughter of František Duchwald, also a citizen of Soběslav. Andreas and Anna were married by Josephus Walter in the presence of Gregorio Brausek-[?], Adalberto Bilek, and Strobová, the "honour virginie" and daughter of Jacob Strobi, also a citizen of Soběslav.[142] Only two children are known to have been born to Andreas and Anna, Martin {Matrinus} and Mathias.

Martin {Matrinus} Příhoda was born in Soběslav on 04 October 1753. He was baptized there by the Catholic Vicar Franc Anger. The godfather was Antonius Weismann and the witnesses were Wenceslaus Frestl and Marie Anna, wife of Ignác Frestl. All were citizens of Soběslav.[143]

On 07 February 1780, when he was twenty-seven years old, Martin Příhoda married Anna (or Marie-Anna) Cilková. The rites of marriage were performed by Wenceslaus Rieb, also a Vicar of the Catholic Church, at Nedvědice No. 24, presumably the home of the bride. Witnesses at the wedding were Carolus Hermon and Thomas Hertz, both citizens of Soběslav. As may be seen on the map in Figure I-5, Nedvědice is a small village about 4 km (= 2-$\frac{1}{2}$ miles) northwest of Soběslav. It is noteworthy that both the bride and groom are recorded as free citizens, not "serfdomers."[144,145] Martin Prihoda's profession was listed as that of a brick maker,[146] and later as a cobbler.[147]

The bride, Anna Cilková, named Marie-Anna at birth, was the daughter of Ignatius Cilek and Marianna Neškodná, both serfdomers of the manor Soběslav. Anna was born in the village of Klenovice, about 2 km (= 2-$\frac{1}{4}$ miles) north of Soběslav. [See Fig. I-5.] Her paternal grandfather had been a shepherd.[148]

During the nine year period from 1786 to 1795, Martin and Anna became parents to six children. All were born free "from the village of Nedvědice No. 24." The eldest of these was their son, Jan, who was born on 31 May 1786 "...free (not the serfdomer), Catholic, male, and from the legal bed..."[149]   Jan's godfather was Mr. Joseph Ferra, the councilman; the midwife attending the birth was Františka Stiborová.

On 02 November 1796, at the age of thirty-eight, Marie-Anna (née Cilková) Příhodova died from "the fever." Martin continued on for another forty-six years. On 22 July 1842, at the age of eighty-six years, he too passed away. Martin Příhoda was buried two days later by P. Mathias Solberg, the Localist.

As noted above, Jan Příhoda was born a freeman from the village of Nedvědice No. 24 on 31 May 1786. Thirty-four years later, Jan took a bride, Sofie {Žofie} Freslová, the nineteen year old daughter of Karel Fressl, the draper, and Voršila (née Ferrová) from the town Soběslav No. 34. Jan followed in his father's footsteps; he too was recorded as the village brick maker. Over the decade beginning in 1821, Jan and Sofie had seven children.

Fifth Generation

Karel Prihoda (1831 - ?)

The youngest child of Jan and Sofie was Karel Příhoda. Karel was born and baptized in 1831 in the village of Nedvědice No. 24. [It is of interest to note that copies of the birth records of Karel Příhoda were issued four times: first on 24 May 1859, then twice in 1940 and once in 1941.]

According to Příhoda family lore, Karel was a teacher and dentist. Extant records show that he was the lower teacher at the parish school in the village of Velká Chýška.[150] This is the first record showing a member of the Příhoda family outside the immediate vicinity of Soběslav. What caused Karel to relocate to the town of Velká Chýška, about 38 km (or 24 miles) northeast of Soběslav, remains an open question. [See Fig. I-5.]

Official extant records show that Karel married twice.[151] These wives of Karel Příhoda were sisters: Františka Moravcová and Johanna Moravcová, daughters of Josef Moravec and Johanna Matoušová. They both were born in the home of the Moravecs, Velká Chýška No. 2, Františka in 1831 and Johanna in 1834.[152] Their father, Josef Moravec was also a teacher at the parish school in Velká Chýška. Perhaps it was through a possible liaison between Karel and Josef at the parish school, that Karel came to meet the Moravec sisters.

Karel Příhoda married Františka first, probably about 1855, judging from the ages of their children. Actually their first child, Karolina Příhodova, born on 23 September 1855, was illegitimate, but later Karel declared that he was the father.[153] About twelve years later, after giving birth to five more children, Františka died; this was on 03 September 1866. Eight months later, on 21 May 1867, Karel married Johanna Moravcová and six months after that, on 25 November 1867, the first of their four children was born. During much of this period, Karel's home in Velká Chýška seems to have moved around. Births of his children were recorded from Velká Chýška No. 2 (the home of his father-in-law) in 1855; No. 15 in 1857; No. 25 in 1859 and 1861; and No. 54 in 1863, 1865, 1867, and 1870; and No. 25 again in 1872 and 1875.

According to a Bible record kept by his daughter, Matylda Příhodova, Karel, married a third time.[154] This third wife has been identified from the christening records of Velká Chýška as Wilhelmina Konečná, a teacher from Hořepnik No. 80 and the daughter of Antonin Konečny. Karel and Wilhilmina had only one child, a daughter. On 09 February 1888, Marie Apolena Prihodova was christened.[155]

David Kohout, a professional genealogist from Prague hired by the author to research the family's extant records in the Czech Republic, found one detail of particular interest. The maternal grandmother of both Františka Moravcová and Johanna Moravcová was Karolina Drkavová. Karolina was the daughter of Jakub Drkava, who was "the director in Prague."

Fig. IV-1. Karel Prihoda (1861 - ?) as a young man.

Fig. IV-2. Karel Prihoda in his senior years. On the reverse side of the photograph the following is printed: "Josef Heidlm z PRAHY aus Prag."

Fig. IV-3. Jana (née Moravcová) Prihodova, second wife of Karel Prihoda

Sixth Generation

Jan Prihoda (1859-1939)

Jan Prihoda was the third child of Karel Prihoda and his first wife, Františeka Moravcova. He was born on 31 May 1859 in Pelhrimov, Velká Chýška, Bohemia and died on 22 November 1939. Jan was a stationary engineer in Prague and worked first on a complex of buildings on Sofie's {Zofin} Island in the center of the city. Later, he was appointed chief engineer of the Obchodni Banka Building at the corner of the famous Wenceslaw Square and Vodickova Street {Ulice}. In the eyes of his grandson, Josef Masek, Jan was a genius in his trade.[156]

Fig. IV-4. Karolina (née Kresslova) Prihodova (center) and her daughters, Wilma (left) and Sofie.

On 21 February 1881 in Pilsen, Bohemia, Jan married Karolina Kresslova and during the period from 1882 to 1888, they had six children. Their two youngest children were daughters named Marie and Wilhelma. Around 1910 in Prague, Marie married Karel Masek. Marie and Karel were parents to eight children, all born in Prague.

Bedrick Prihoda (1867-1948)

Bedrick (or "Fredrick") Prihoda was the first child of Karel Prihoda and his second wife, Johanna née Moravcova. According to the 1900 U.S. census,[157] Bedrick came to America in 1890, worked as a locksmith, lived with his family at 144 West 18th Place in Chicago, and could not speak English. According to the family Bible, Bedrick was born 25 November 1867 in Bohemia and died on 01 January 1948 in Michigan City, Indiana. On 04 June 1888 in Chicago, Bedrick married Mary Balvin (or Balwin), the daughter of Joseph Balvin (or Balwin).[158] Also from the 1900 census,[159] Mary and both her parents were born in Bohemia and Mary came to America in 1885. Bedrick and Mary had four children, all born in Chicago: Jennie, Charles, Jaroslav (later anglicized to Jerome), and Peter.

On Monday, 28 April 1913, Jennie Prihoda married, at 1510 West 18th Street, Chicago, Illinois, George Kripner. In the 1920 census, George's occupation is given as shipping clerk for an automotive company. He and Jennie are recorded as renters at 1615 Karlov Avenue in Chicago with four children: Fred, Emily, George, and Jerome.[160] One son was killed at an early age in a motorcycle accident; Emily married and moved to California; another son relocated to southern New Jersey. Jerome (or Gerald) died in Illinois in 1983.[161]

Fig. IV-5. Peter Prihoda (left) and Bliss Franchowski circa 1926-27.

Charles Prihoda married Mary Malicka, born 19 December 1898 in Prague, Bohemia, the daughter of August and Marketa Malicka; died 20 March 1989 in Michigan City.[162] At the time of her marriage to Charles, Mary was a widow with two children from her former marriage. Charles and Mary did not have any children.[163] Mary's daughter, Georgia Law, married Arthur G. Utpatel and with him lived at 2410 Oak Street, Michigan City, Indiana.[164]

Fig. IV-6. Envelope addressed to "Mrs. M. Rucker, Little Ferry, New Jersey, from Mrs. Jennie Kripner, 1615 So. Karlov Ave., Chicago, Ills."

Jerome Prihoda served as a Private in the U.S. Army during World War I. He enlisted on 08 December 1917 in Indianapolis, Indiana and was discharged on 29 December 1918 at Camp Sherman in Ohio.[165] He also worked for a time in New Jersey, during which he stayed with his aunt, Matylda (née Prihodova) Rucker. Late in life, Jerome married Leona (née Barnett) Law, a widow who had two children from her previous marriage, Keith Law and Frances Law.[166] [Frances married Grant Smith.] Jerry and Leona lived at 1619 Eighth Street, Michigan City, Indiana where they raised and sold geranium plants.[167]

Fig. IV-7. Jerome Prihoda taken 26 April 1918 in Newport News, Virginia.

The following message is written on the back of the photograph to his Aunt Matylda:

Newport News, Va.
April 26, 1918

Dear Aunt,

Having finally got it and am sending it
with the best of love to you Aunt Matylda.

Your loving nephew,
(signed) Jerome

In 1947, Wilhelma (née Prihodova) Maier, the daughter of Jan Prihoda and Karolina Kresslova, then living in Prague, sent a letter to Leona (née Barnett) (Law) Prihoda. Wilhelma and Leona's husband, Jerome, were first cousins. Below is a copy of the beginning of the letter, written in Czech:

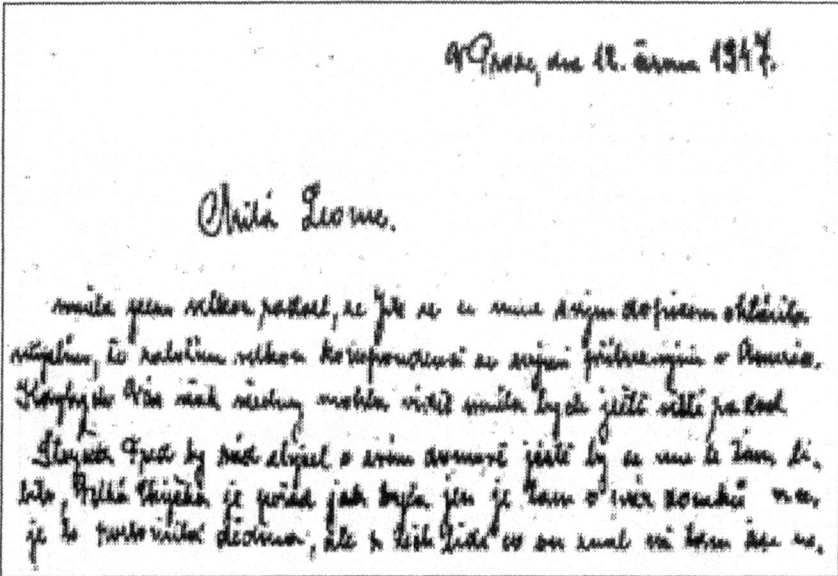

Fig. IV-8. Portion of a letter from Wilhelma (née Prihodova) Maier to Leona (née Barnett) (Law) Prihoda.

A complete translation of the letter from Czech into English follows:

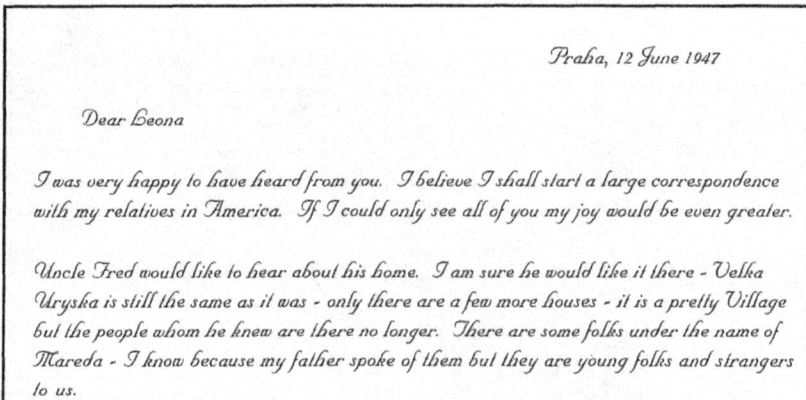

Praha, 12 June 1947

Dear Leona

I was very happy to have heard from you. I believe I shall start a large correspondence with my relatives in America. If I could only see all of you my joy would be even greater.

Uncle Fred would like to hear about his home. I am sure he would like it there - Velka Uryska is still the same as it was - only there are a few more houses - it is a pretty village but the people whom he knew are there no longer. There are some folks under the name of Mareda - I know because my father spoke of them but they are young folks and strangers to us.

My Uncle Charles lived here in Praha. He was my father's brother and a teacher here and later a Prof. in a girl's institution. He lived well but he was an old bachelor when he married. He had one daughter and very shortly afterward became divorced - his wife was much younger than he and then he took his elderly housekeeper as a maid and not long afterward became ill and died. He was a good man and visited us very often. He had dinner with us every Sunday and then we would all go walking down the most beautiful parts of Praha and vicinity. He lived to show us off because he had no children of his own.

My father John, or Honzik, had 6 children - 1 son and 5 daughters. The son's name was Frank and the first daughter's name was Karlicka. At that time my parents liven in Pilsen and because of the diphtheria epidemic both children died. Then my parents moved to Praha and there were born 4 daughters - Sophie, Vilma (that's me), Rose & Marie. There are no male progeny - only women. Sophie's husband was a Bansky engineer (a school for mining engineers) and she has one daughter. Sophie is divorced - she lives very well with her daughter who works in a bank. My husband was a railroad engineer - we had two sons and a daughter (one of my sons died) and in 1943 my husband died of a heart attack (Angina Pectoris). Rose's husband was a sculptor but she was divorced after 3 years and is now manager of a large fashion salon. The youngest, Marie, is married to a tavern keeper and she has 8 children - 4 boys and 4 girls- their name is Masek. So there is no one carrying the name of Prihoda. We women spoiled it all - there is nothing we can do about it - the main thing is that we are all healthy. My daughter Marketa has 2 boys - 4 years and 2 years and now she is expecting in November. She hopes for a daughter so I am wondering if her wish will come true.

Write me, dear Leona, something about your husband and yourself - how old is he and what is his occupation - in fact everything about all the Prihodas living in America. I believe there was in America also Uncle Theodore - they called him Dorik - and he ended very tragically - How many offspring remained

You too have a small grandchild - write me how old he is. I am sorry that Uncle Fred is so helpless - be good to him. If he would have a repeated attack, it would be bad. You write how dear he is to you and I am sorry I never knew him. Please give him my best regards. When you write again tell me all about Karel (Charles) and Peter so I know something about them.

You write about Bohumil Haralik from Praha - I am not acquainted with him but if he should come to Praha I would like to talk to him about you - at least I would get to know something more about you.

Please extend to all Prihodas and their families my most sincere regards.

With Love,
Wilma

Matylda (née Prihodova) Rucker (1875-1947)

Matylda Prihodova was born on Monday, 15 March 1875 in Velká Chýška, Bohemia, the fourth child of Karel's second wife, Johanna.[168] Little is known of her early life. Her mother, Johanna, died when Matylda was seven and, according to family lore, she was not treated well by her step-mother, the third wife of Karel Prihoda, Wilhelmina (née Konečná) Prihodova.

Fig. IV-9. Matylda Prihoda in her early twenties.[169]

As a young woman, Matylda left the family home at in Velká Chýška No. 25 and went to live with an older brother and his wife in Prague. While in Prague, Matylda learned of an American woman who became ill while visiting

Prague and needed someone to care for her during her return trip to the United States. Matylda was that person. Not long after her arrival in America, Matylda took a job as a cook at the home of a jeweler in New York City. The jeweler, his family, and Matylda spent one or two summers at a vacation resort in the Catskill Mountains, near the town of Liberty, New York. Sometime after that, Matylda met Mrs. Bohirmir (or Bohnue) Vevera, the sister of the woman for whom Matylda cared during the ocean crossing. Mrs. Vevera resided at 52 Garden Street in Little Ferry, New Jersey. And it was she who introduced Matylda to Adolf Rücker. Within the year, Matylda and Adolf were married — the wedding took place on Sunday, 03 July 1904 in Manhattan, New York City, New York.

For the first two years of their marriage, Matylda and Adolf lived in Little Ferry on Garden Street, on the second floor, in the home of Mrs. Vevera. On 17 January 1906, their first child was born: Carolina, later called "Carrie." Now needing a home of their own, on 28 September 1906, Adolf and Matylda jointly purchased from Alexander Hettenbach, a single man, and Catharina Joekli, a widow, the house at 135 Washington Avenue, Little Ferry. The cost for this house and the land on which it stood was $1500.[170] Two-thirds of this money was borrowed from Hypolit and Anna Paroubek.[171]

For reasons of preserving the family history, the legal description of that property follows:[172]

Description of Property: Beginning in the Southerly line of the road leading from Little Ferry to Moonachie [Washington Avenue] and in the North-east corner of land (formerly of Martin Hartwick); thence running southerly along the Easterly line formerly of Martin Hartwick, One Hundred and Eighty (180) feet, more or less, to land of the Mehrhoff Brothers, thence Easterly along line of Mehrhoff Brothers, Thirty-six (36) feet to the Westerly line of land of Carl and Barbara Rucker and thence Northerly along the same and in a line parallel with the first, One Hundred and eighty feet, more or less, to the Southerly line of said Road; and thence Westerly along the same, Thirty-six (36) feet to the point or place of the beginning.

Being the same premises conveyed to the said Alexander der Hettenbach and Catharina Joekli, by deed dated May the Fifteenth, Nineteen Hundred and Two (1902) recorded in the Bergen County Clerk's office May the Seventeenth, Nineteen Hundred and Two (1902).

Fig. IV-10. Rucker Family home at 135 Washington Avenue, Little Ferry, NJ
(Photo taken 09 May 1997.)

That house at 135 Washington Avenue was the birthplace for the rest of the children of Adolf and Matylda. Over the next four years, four more children were added to the family: Mary in 1907, Frances in 1908, Edward in 1909, and Adolph (also known as "Otto" and "Bep")[173] in 1910. A sixth child, named after her mother, was born on 15 March 1917. Sadly, infant Matylda Rucker died from pneumonia just twenty-five days after her birth. She was interred in the family plot on 09 April 1917, the day after Easter Sunday.[174]

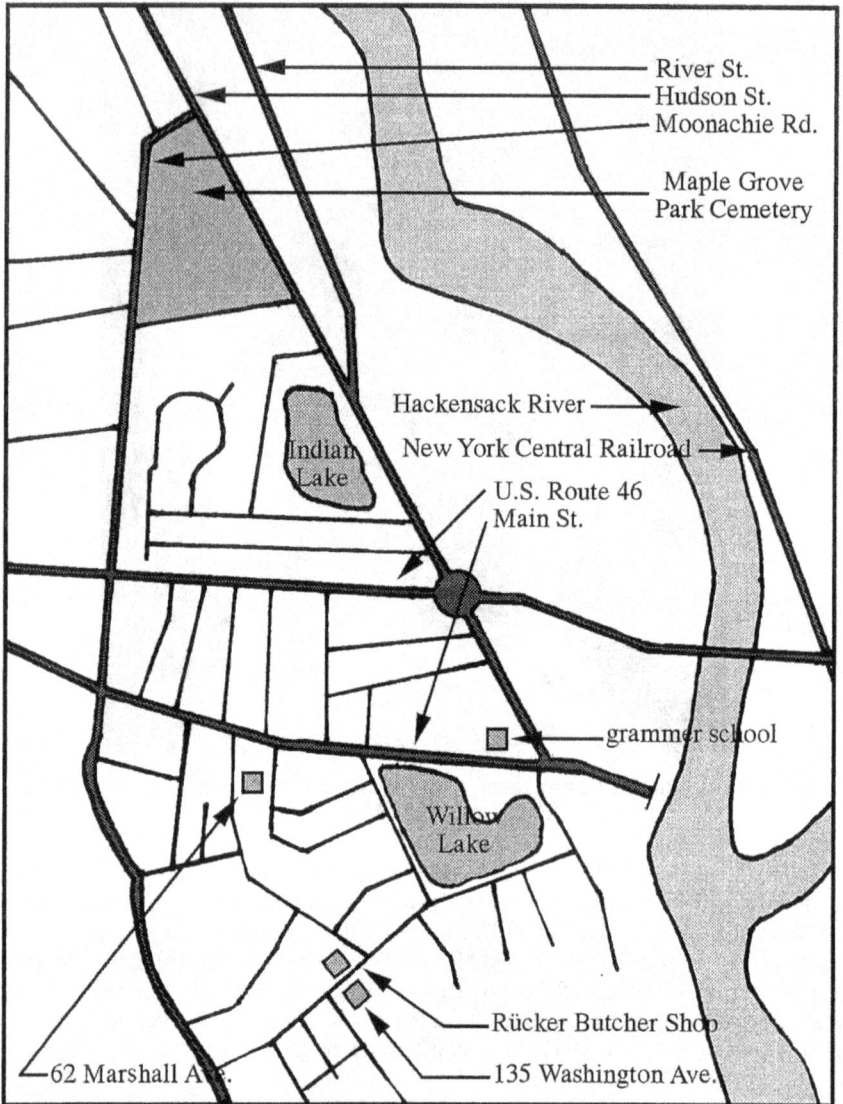

River St.
Hudson St.
Moonachie Rd.

Maple Grove
Park Cemetery

Hackensack River
New York Central Railroad
U.S. Route 46
Main St.

Indian Lake

grammer school

Willow Lake

Rücker Butcher Shop
62 Marshall Ave.
135 Washington Ave.

Fig. IV-11. Map showing some of the streets of Little Ferry and Hackensack, New Jersey. Maple Grove Cemetery is in the upper left; the Rucker family home and butcher shop are in the lower center.

Adolf's daughters have a benevolent recollection of their father's personality: Frances says that she did not know him very well. He left home early in the morning and returned late at night. But she does recall times of his entertaining the family with his accordion playing and singing. Apparently he had an exceptional singing voice. He sang with a group at the Delnicka Americah Sokol Hall (= "Working Americans Social Hall") in Little Ferry. The Sokol Hall was the center of activity in the Bohemian community in Little Ferry.

In response to a question of what church her parents attended, daughter Mary recounted the following incident: While still in Bohemia, her father was serving as an alter boy. There was an occasion when the priest caught young Adolf and another alter boy drinking the sacramental wine. Both boys were then summarily ordered out of the church by the priest. In retaliation, Adolf vowed never to set foot in a church again. According to family lore, he honored his vow.

The three daughters each were baptized as infants at a Catholic church in the adjacent town of Hackensack. The church was originally called St. Mary's, but, when officially incorporated on 05 June 1891, it was under the name of the Church of the Immaculate Conception, as it is known today.[175] Carolina was baptized on 29 April 1906 and her younger sisters, Mary and Frances, on 02 August 1908.[176] The sponsor for each sister was their aunt, Barbara (née Kukal) Rücker.

The Church of the Immaculate Conception

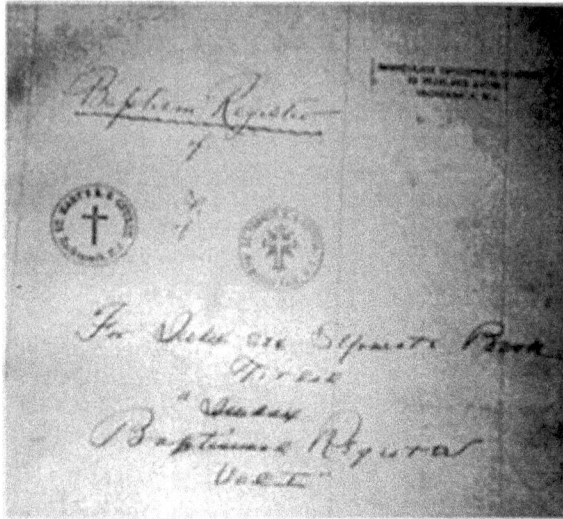

Fig. IV-12. Front page of the first Baptismal Record
Book of the Church of the Immaculate Conception.

This church was established in 1891 when Reverend John Hennes was appointed the first resident pastor of St. Mary's, as the new church was first called. However it was officially incorporated on 05 June 1891 under the name of the Church of the Immaculate Conception.

There are two sets of records in this church that contain information about the Rucker family: baptismal and marriage.

Baptismal Records

There are two official seals on the above baptismal record. The first, on the left in Figure IV-12, reads: "ST. MARY'S R. C. [Roman Catholic] CHURCH, Hackensack, N.J."; the second, on the right, says: "ST. FRANCIS R. C. [Roman Catholic] CHURCH, Ridgefield Park, N.J."

The baptismal records in this book contain the following information: baptismal number, father's name, mother's name, child's name, date of birth, date of baptism, sponsor's name, and priest's name. A copy of a photograph of the baptismal record of Mary and Frances Rucker, as recorded on page 69 of the church register on 02 August 1908 is shown in Figure IV-13.

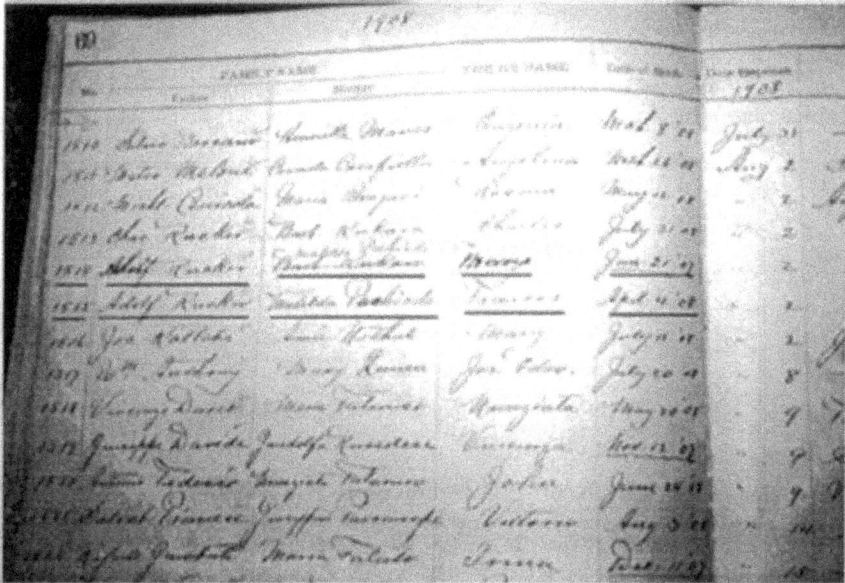

Fig. IV-13. Copy of a photograph of the upper part of page 69 showing the official record of the Church of the Immaculate Conception of the baptism of Mary and Frances Rucker, Nos. 1514 and 1515, respectively, on 02 August 1908. (The underlining was added by the author; it is not in the original document.)

A transcription of the Rucker family records in this baptismal register follows:

Pg	No.	Father	Mother	Name	Birth Date	Bapt. Date	Sponsor
46	966	Charles Rucker	Barbara Gugal	William	28 Oct. 1903	03 Jul. 1904	Wm. Weleck
54	1166	Adolf Rucker	Mat. Prihoda	Carolina	17 Jan. 1906	29 Apr. 1906	Barb. Rucker
69	1513	Charles Rucker	Barb. Kukara	Charles	31 Jul. 1908	02 Aug. 1908	Chas. Weleck
69	1514	Adolf Rucker	Mat. Prihoda ~~Barb. Rucker~~	Mary	21 Jan. 1907	02 Aug. 1908	Barb. Rucker
69	1515	Adolf Rucker	Mat. Prihoda	Frances	04 Apr. 1908	02 Aug. 1908	Barb. Rucker

Abbreviations used in the above table are: Barb. = Barbara; Chas. = Charles; Mat. = Matylda; Wm. = William. It is noted that in the original document, the name of the mother of Mary Rucker was first written as Barbara Rucker, her aunt and sponsor. A line is drawn through that name and the correct name, "Mat. Prihoda," is written above. It also is noted that both the left leaf and right leaf in this book carry the same page number. The last column is not reproduced in the above table. It contains the name of the priest and in all cases is the same, "J. E. Lambert."

Marriage Records

The front cover of Volume 1 of the Marriage Register of the Church of the Immaculate Conception carries the following inscription:

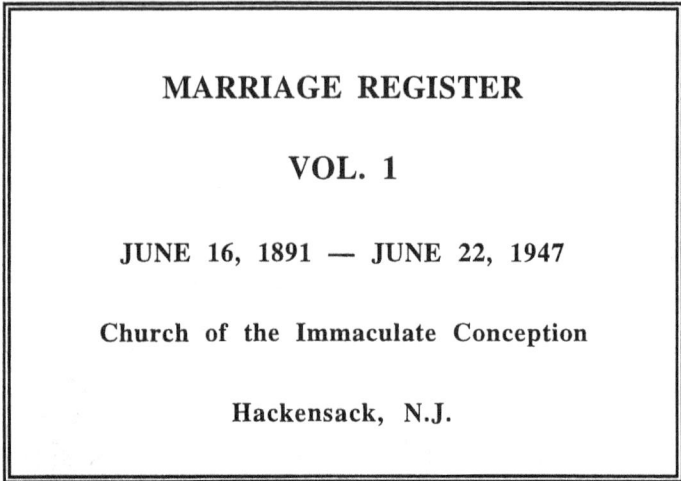

MARRIAGE REGISTER

VOL. 1

JUNE 16, 1891 — JUNE 22, 1947

Church of the Immaculate Conception

Hackensack, N.J.

The type of information recorded in this register is as follows: marriage number, groom's name, bride's name, date of marriage, names of two witnesses (usually a male and a female), and priest's name. Figure IV-14 is a copy of a photograph of the 24 July 1927 record for the marriage of Rudolph Komarek and Carolina Rucker, as recorded on page 28 of the marriage record.

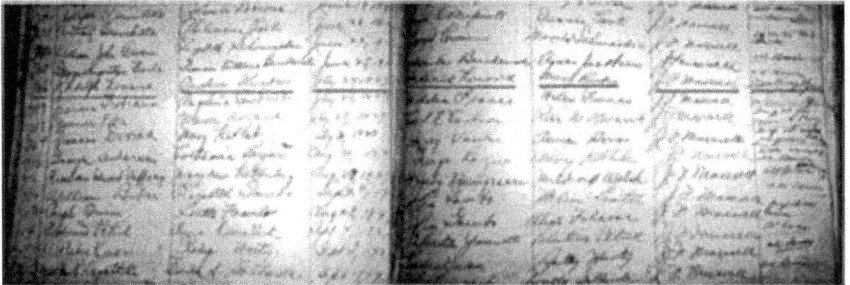

Fig. IV-14. Copy of a photograph of the lower part of page 28 of the marriage records of the Church of the Immaculate Conception. The record of the marriage between Rudolph Komarek and Carolina Rucker, No. 706, on 24 July 1927, has been underscored. (The underlining was added by the author; it is not in the original document.)

Why the sons were not also baptized as infants is not known. A possible reason is that Matylda disliked the forename "Adolf" and would not christen her younger son as such. On the other hand, Adolf wanted to see his name carried into the next generation. The result may have been a stalemate as nothing happened.

Son Edward was baptized when he was thirty-three years old. This was in the fall or winter of 1942, just before his induction into the Army and World War II. However, there is no record of this at the Church of the Immaculate Conception.[177]

Fig. IV-15. Matylda (née Prihodova) Rucker taken circa 1945 in Little Ferry, NJ

Seventh Generation

<u>Early Years of the Children of Adolf and Matylda Rucker</u>

Fig. IV-16. Carrie Rucker at about 11
years of age.

Fig. IV-17. Mary Rucker at about 10
years of age.

On the bottom of the original photograph of Edward in Fig. IV-19, the following information is printed: "L. Kieffer, Photographer, 67 Teaneck Road, Ridgefield Park, N.J." On the back of the original snapshot of Fig. IV-20 is the following hand written text, "Baby Rucker Kindergarten." This probably was written by his mother, Matylda. His nickname, "Bep," is derived from "Baby" and the fact that he was the youngest of the five siblings. Later, when meeting people, he called himself "Roy."

Carrie was the oldest of the Rucker children. To her father, she was the "apple of his eye;" to her siblings, she was the "most pampered and spoiled." As the eldest, she always received the new clothes; others received "hand-me-downs," as the clothes made their way down the birth chain. An unfortunate result of this natural "pecking order" was a sense of alienation that seemed to grow between Carrie and her younger sisters and brothers. As the years passed, the schism widened. Frances recalled one particularly ugly incident when, as a child she was "caught" by Carrie playfully wearing a pair of high heel shoes with bows which Carrie considered hers. (The shoes had been passed down from their cousins, Mary and Carrie Rucker, as they had outgrown them.) Carrie pulled the shoes off Fannie's feet and began beating her with them, mercilessly. Fortunately, Mary intervened before the beating went too far.

Fig. IV-19. Edward Rucker in first grade (ca. 1915).

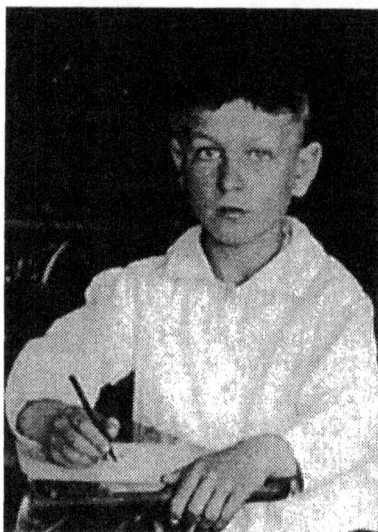

Fig. IV-18. Frances Rucker in first grade (ca. 1914).

The grammar school located on Main Street in Little Ferry was attended by the Rucker children of both Charles and Barbara and of Adolf and Matylda. [See map in Fig. IV-11.] The building no longer exists.

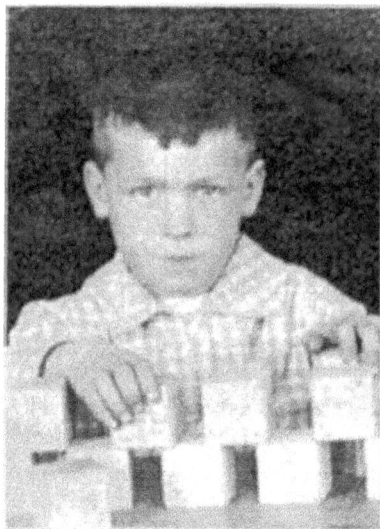

Fig. IV-20. Adolph Rucker in kindergarten (ca. 1915).

Fig. IV-21. Adolph Rucker on front steps of family home on Washington Avenue circa 1915.

Fig. IV-22. Five Rucker siblings: Carrie, Edward, Adolph, Mary, and Frances. (Photograph taken by Jerome Prihoda circa 1917.)

On the back of the photograph in Figure IV-22 is the following inscription, *"Jerry, who was drafted in WW-I, came to visit in 1917. Rabbit coop and outhouse in rear. Empty lot where we & neighbors' kids played a lot."* "Jerry" is Jerome Prihoda and is pictured in Figure IV-7 in his World War I uniform. This photo also probably was taken circa 1917 - 1918.

The graduation of the children from elementary school (eighth grade) into high school was a memorable event. Below are graduation photographs of Mary and Frances and a photo of Carrie from the same period.

In the early 1920's, when the Rucker children were in their late teen years, most were working — in addition to attending high school. Mary, Frances, and Edward worked for Dr. Groff, a medical doctor serving the community. Mary worked in his office as a receptionist after school and, Eddie drove the doctor on his house calls. Frances substituted for Mary from time to time and helped her brother attend to the gardening on Saturdays. [It is of interest to note that Dr. Groff also delivered all the children of Carrie, Mary, and Frances.]

Fig. IV-23. Carrie Rucker as a teenager.

Fig. IV-24. Mary Rucker upon graduation from elementary school, circa 1921.

Fig. IV-25. Frances Rucker upon graduation from
elementary school, circa 1922.

The Rucker sons never married; the daughters married in two year intervals:
Carrie to Rudolph Komarek in 1927, Mary to William Franklin Frotscher in
1929, and Frances to Floyd Skelton in 1931.

Carolina (née Rucker) Komarek (1906-1962)

On Wednesday, 17 January 1906, Carolina, or "Carrie" as she was known to family and friends, was born on Garden Street in Little Ferry, in the home of Mrs. Vevera. Several months later, her parents moved into the family home on Washington Avenue. When in her teens, Carrie delivered mail for people and cleaned house for a doctor in the neighborhood. A time later, she worked in a bank in Little Ferry and in the 1920's, she worked in New York City as a computing machine operator.

Fig. IV-26. Rudolph Komarek, Matylda (née Prihoda) Rucker, Carrie (née Rucker) Komarek, and Adolf Rucker at the Rucker family home on 24 July 1927.

On Sunday, 24 July 1927, Carrie married Rudolph Komarek. The exchange of nuptials took place at St. Margaret's Church on Washington Avenue in Little Ferry.[178] Rudolph, or "Rudy," as he was called, also was of Czech ancestry. Like the Prihodas, the Komareks also came from the Bohemian portion of what was then the northwestern portion of the Austrian Empire. Rudy was born in Europe on 05 October 1903.

Fig. IV-27. Mary Rucker, Rudolph Komarek,
Frederick Komarek (a cousin of Rudolph),
and Carrie (née Rucker) Komarek on 24 July 1927.

When a small boy, Rudy immigrated to America with his family, arriving
on the vessel *America* at the Port on New York on 05 October 1903. In his
Declaration of Intention to become a U.S. citizen, Rudy reported that he was
born in Krompach, Czechoslovakia and that his last residence in Europe had been
in Boynice, Czechoslovakia.[179] At first the Komareks lived in the Borough of
New York City, where his father worked as a baker. Some years later, the
family moved to a house at 62 Marshall Avenue in Little Ferry.[180] [See map
in Fig. IV-11.] The move from New York to the more pastoral lands of
northern New Jersey, as they were then, may have been influenced by the
Petriks, relatives of the Komareks, who already lived in the town. While
growing up in New Jersey, Rudy learned the electricians trade and became a
naturalized citizen of the United States.[181]

Fig. IV-28. Rudolph and Carrie Komarek in 1926.

After his marriage, Rudy opened an electrical supply store on Washington Avenue, not far from the family home on Marshall Avenue. Unfortunately this was during the time of the Great Depression and the business eventually failed. Perhaps one factor contributing to its demise is the corruption that seemed to prevail throughout the area at the time. His son, Robert, recalled an incident in which his father was bidding on a job for the installation of fire alarm boxes on the streets of Little Ferry. The contract for the work was awarded to a competitor of his father. The winning bid was exactly one dollar lower than Rudy's — clearly the sealed bids had not remained so.

Rudy then worked at whatever jobs he could find. Among these were collecting trash and working on the roads for the WPA, the Work Projects Administration. Eventually Rudolph Komarek made his way out of debt and put his family back on their feet. In time, he was able to join the International

Brotherhood of Electrical Workers in New York City. That, coupled with his natural acumen for good jobs and a head for business, led to a very lucrative life style. [On 10 June 1985, the International Brotherhood of Electrical Workers awarded Rudolph Komarek a pin and a citation, and extended their deep gratitude for his sixty-five years of membership.]

Fig. IV-29. Rudolph Komarek in 1951

Fig. IV-30. Carrie (née Rucker) Komarek in 1951

A glimpse into his adventuresome personality is provided by a story recalled by his nephew, Bill Frotscher: "...a broken wooden propeller hung on the corner of his garage. I was told that sometime during the 1920's he [Rudy] had taken to flying an airplane. On one occasion something went wrong. Supposedly all that was left of the plane was the broken propeller. Whether the story was true or false I never did find out. He wouldn't talk about anything he didn't wish to and furthermore, he wouldn't allow himself to be forced into saying anything he didn't want to say. These conversations usually ended with his dismissing the subject and saying, 'Oh, that's just nonsense,' or maybe just flat 'nonsense.' After which he would fold his arms, clear his throat, and often with a smile on his face, start another conversation on another topic..." Rudy also was an accomplished glider pilot and a member of the Soaring Society of America.[182]

As the years passed and the financial status of the family improved, the Komareks relocated from their home on Marshall Avenue in Little Ferry to one in Ridgewood, a town in a more affluent part of Bergen County, about eight miles northwest of Little Ferry. This new home, located at 281 Van Emburgh

Avenue, was one that Rudy had built, with help from the family. Rudy also purchased a large cabin cruiser which was kept at the prestigious Englewood Yacht Basin, located on the Hudson River, below the Palisade Cliffs.

Carrie passed away on 27 July 1962, following a protracted bout with cancer. Her remains are interred in the George Washington Memorial Park Cemetery in Paramus, New Jersey. After his retirement, Rudy sold the Ridgewood home to his younger son, Robert, and purchased a home in the resort community of Jekyll Island, on Georgia's Atlantic coast.[183] He married twice after Carrie's passing. The forename of his second wife was Viola; his third wife was Miriam Dorr. Rudy died on 20 February 1987 in Louisville, Kentucky from cardiopulmonary arrest, brought on by empyema seizures. His remains were returned to New Jersey and are buried in the George Washington Memorial Park Cemetery, near those of his first wife, Carrie.[184]

Fig. IV-31. Last photograph of the three Rucker sisters together.
From left to right: Frances Skelton, Carrie Komarek, and Mary Frotscher.
The photograph was taken on 17 June 1962 in Hackensack, New Jersey.

Mary (née Rucker) Frotscher (1907-   )

Regretfully, the Rucker girls were not encouraged to continue their education. Mary recalls, "My mother said two years [of high school] was enough. Let someone else go."[185] So, at 17-$^1/_2$ years of age, Mary dropped out of Hackensack High School and entered nursing school at the Hackensack Hospital. Two and one-half years later, she graduated as a Registered Nurse. She then served as a private nurse and was appointed as a school nurse in Moonachie, N.J.

On 09 July 1929 in Newport, Kentucky, Mary married William Franklin Frotscher, known to friends and family as "Bud." Bud was born on 11 October 1903 in Bellevue, Campbell County, Kentucky, the son of Herman C. Frotscher and Elizabeth Bareswelt, both German immigrants. Bellevue is a small town in northern Kentucky, located across the Ohio River from Cincinnati. One of Bud's first jobs was as a copyboy for the *Cincinnati Enquirer*. He worked his way up to police reporter, before leaving the area to join his mother, who had temporarily relocated to Little Ferry.

During his senior years, Bud spent some time recollecting and recording the memoirs of a lifetime. Some of these he put on paper and some on audio tape. Recently his son, William Franklin Frotscher, Jr., took the initiative of compiling these stories, notes, and tapes into a book entitled *Dad's Stories Tales of Growing up on the banks of the Ohio and other stories*. A copy of Chapter 16 from that work follows. It contains the very interesting saga of the Bud Frotscher's life with *The Cincinnati Enquirer*.[186]

CHAPTER 16

THE CINCINNATI ENQUIRER

A long time friend of the family was a reporter on the *Cincinnati Enquirer*. My oldest brother, Herman, and he got together one day. While discussing what various members of the family were doing, the friend told my brother that there was an opening for a copyboy on the newspaper. They both felt it was an excellent opportunity for me, and certainly held much more promise than what I was doing at Pat Parrish's junk yard. Word was left with my brother, that if I applied right away I could have the job. I had no idea at all what the work entailed, but I applied and I was hired. At that time I was 18 years old and it was, indeed, time for me to chose a life's work. Unfortunately, this did not prove to be the end of the job changes and challenges in searching for a job that might promise security.

The work of a copyboy was varied and interesting, and never dull. I quickly became interested in the work and tried my best to do a good job. The work was very hectic as was life, in general, about the newspaper. At this place in time, the newspaper was the prime news media. Radio & television were only playthings with which very few people were even familiar. Telephones were in use at that time. Only few could afford to use them and, for the most part that was for business and emergency use. A system of public telephones had been developed around the cities, and this became the main method of getting information to the newspaper from the reporters out in the street. The teletype was available for communication with the news services for inter-city communication of national and international news. One of my early duties was to answer some of the telephones which seemed to be ringing almost continuously. Prior to getting this job I had only talked on a telephone once or twice, and I was very reluctant to try to carry on a conversation with someone who I couldn't even see. But, one of the requirements of the job was to answer the calls and then try to get someone who was familiar with the nature of the call to take their messages. After a while I became used to the phones, and before too long I learned to type and take stories as they were called in.

The primary job of the copyboys was to run errands. "Copy," or written information, had to be transported from one department to another. Often it was vitally important that the information be transported quickly as "press time" became close. The newspaper worked on a very regimented scheduled that required specific things be done by a certain time, if the newspaper was to get out on the streets on time. Usually, the first paper to get out on the street with a breaking story would be the one to sell the most copies, and, for sure, selling papers was the name of the game.

There were a half dozen or more people in the department where I first worked. Three copyboys were easily kept busy "running copy," and if there wasn't any copy to run, then there were the many trips for coffee and donuts, or sandwiches, or whatever may be needed at the time. Sometimes we even had to go out to the street and buy a competitor's paper to see what they were printing.

One of the regular trips we had to make was to the office of the Hearst Wire-Service which provided us with information of what was happening in New York, as well as in many other places around the world. The wire-service office was located on the fourth floor of the Palace Hotel which was a few blocks away from our building. Our bosses well knew how long it took to get back and forth between the offices. We were expected to run at top speed whereever we went. Promptness was rewarded. Tardiness was grounds for dismissal, or, at the least, rebuff.

Since I was single while working at the paper, I was given a job working on the night shift. The elevator stopped running after ten o'clock at the Palace Hotel which meant we had to use the stairs. While going up we would skip three or four steps at a time at a full run. Coming down was even more exciting. The stairs were granite, and, from frequent use, became quite slippery. We wore leather sole shoes and, with a little practice, learned to slide down the stairs by just scooting over the edges. We would make a running dive and off we would go from flight to flight much like a water-skier bare-footing over the water surface.

Of course, there were times when things would go wrong and we would go head-over-heels, but in such situations the main concern was to protect the copy. When we finally came to a stop, we would check ourselves over quickly, and if nothing was broken, would quickly be on our way, definitely trying to correct the technique on the next flight of stairs.

Another part of my daily routine involved going to the Federal building to get the weather reports. The two buildings were three or four blocks apart and, rain or shine, one of the copyboys had to make the trip. Again, the trip had to be made at a dead run. Splashing along through the wet city streets wasn't much fun, especially when it was cold and snowy. Usually we were wearing our leather shoes which promptly became soaked, as did the sparse clothing which we wore in an attempt to keep cool while running between the buildings.

The weather bureau closed at 5:00 PM every evening. My shift ran somewhere between 2:00 PM and 2:00 AM. We were only allowed to work for eight hours during that period. So, the copyboys arranged to make a sliding schedule to make sure there was always sufficient help available during the busiest times. Generally, there was adequate time for me to get to the weather bureau from the time I started work until it closed, if I was working during that period. However, the editors always wanted the latest report as close as possible to the 5:00 PM closing, and it always seemed that about this time things were happening all over the world at a frenzied pace. As I recall, my many trips to the Federal building were amongst the most harrying part of my job. No matter what, I had to get there and get the weather report back to the paper. Tens of thousands of people all over the city and surrounding area were anxiously waiting and dependent on this information to help them plan for their next day. There was no other source of the information available.

After working for a year at my position as copyboy I desired to take a vacation. When the City Editor agreed that I probably should have a vacation, and instructed me to find a boy to take my place, I began to worry. I wondered if maybe he had decided to give me a permanent vacation. I cautiously approached him one day and let him know that I really could get along without a vacation, particularly if there was any possibility that my replacement would take my place permanently. He looked at me rather hard, and gruffly replied, "Well actually, that is what I had in mind." My heart skipped a beat and jumped up into my throat. I was afraid that was what he was thinking. But, then a smile came over his face, and he continued, "What I really had in mind was to move you up to a reporter's job, with a ten dollar a week raise!" At that point I was "floating-on-air".

While working as a copyboy, I had tried very hard to do the job of a reporter. I practiced on the typewriter whenever there was a chance, until I became quite fast and accurate. I became able to take stories over the phone as they were called in by the street reporters, and, after a while, I could type as fast as they could tell the story to me, as long as they didn't rush too much. The phone would be propped between my shoulder and ear and my hands would be on the keys, pounding away.

On several occasions I became a reporter in a different fashion. When there was a major news event breaking, crowds would gather in the street in front of the news building. Quite often I would be given a megaphone and would relate the news through the open window to the people waiting below. The most memorable occasion of news relating occurred during the Dempsey - Tunney heavyweight boxing championship [23 September 1926]. After each round I would announce the results, as it would come in over the wire service. In some cases, it was an almost blow by blow description as the reporter at the arena reported it. For many years this fight had been touted as the "fight of the century". There was a lot of money bet by a lot of people. For many people standing outside the window that evening, fortunes were made or lost, depending upon the news I was relating to them. I felt very important that evening, and, indeed, to many I was.

When I returned from my vacation (which was the boat trip up the Kentucky River, related elsewhere), I purchased some very important books to help me in my new undertaking. One which I remember as being the most useful was Roget's *Treasury of Words*. I was given a privilege badge which opened many unlocked doors to me, and was given a copy of the *City Directory*. When I opened it, I found my name listed among the chosen ones. It really gave me a boost. I was also assigned to my own desk, with a name tag on it, and was given my own private typewriter. The telephone which before had been a bane to my existence now became a part of my eyes, ears, hands and speech.

My first assignment as a reporter was to continue what I had been doing as a copyboy. I no longer had to run copy or errands, unless one of my bosses asked me to, which was seldom. As my experience at the job progressed, I was given more and more important stories to write. At first, I would just gather the information which would go to be re-written by the more experienced reporters. After a while, if I wasn't real busy taking information over the phone, the editor would give me a story and ask me to write it. Before long my stories were being published with little or no modifications. In the meantime, there were many stories which came back to my desk time and time again, to be rewritten to fit the space allotted by the City Editor. In general, he liked my style of reporting, but I had to learn to make the reports concise and to the point. Column space was expensive and the stories had to make "good copy".

One of the first outside assignments I received was to fill in for the social editor who was not available for some reason. I was called upon to attend a very fashionable wedding involving some wealthy socialites in town. Before going I was instructed to wear my best attire and to be sure to conduct myself graciously and courteously. I found myself in a situation requiring that I buy myself some clothes which were appropriate for my position. The evening before the wedding I went out and bought a new suit, top-coat (which I still have to this day, by the way) and a fedora type hat; thus preparing myself for a sojourn into society. As a copyboy, casual type street wear was acceptable, but a reporter from the *Enquirer* was expected to be well dressed for all occasions. A little bit of "flash" was acceptable, as long as it was not overdone. I was never a clothes horse, although I admired nice clothes on other people. Several of the older reporters were especially fine dressers, and, at times, I had yearned to be like them. I felt if I could look like them, maybe it would help me in my job to get into places and to help me talk to the right people to get the information I needed for the stories I was writing. As far as I was concerned, the one article of clothing which I felt to be most important as being the mark of a successful reporter was the light, raincoat-type topcoat which nearly all of them wore in rain or shine. A well known brand name was Cravenette. This became the name by which this article of clothing was known, no matter who was the manufacturer. My prime goal was to make sure I had an original which bore the Cravenette label on the inside. Another goal was to obtain a fedora-type hat manufactured by Stetson.

Except when the weather became very warm I always wore my Cravenette and Stetson. One particular occasion, which I will never forget, occurred when I visited The Beverly Hills Country Club, in Covington, Kentucky. The visit was a semi-business, semi-pleasure occasion. One of the older reporters who knew his way around asked me to go along with him one evening to snoop around and see what we could dig up. We were both doing police reporting at the time, and the Beverly Hills was a place where a lot went on which the police were very much interested in knowing. The "Country Club" was one of the few places around which allowed gambling. It was reputed to be owned by the crime syndicate and was regularly frequented by mobsters from all over the northeast. It was not unusual to find Al Capone, or any other of the other big names from the syndicate sitting at some of the tables.

On the evening of the particular occasion which I recall, my friend decided to play one of the slot machines in an effort to appear casual. Besides that, he also enjoyed gambling, and hated to pass up the opportunity to get a shot at the machines. Being fairly new at this sort of thing, I kind of trailed along behind him, trying not to look too conspicuously inexperienced.

Bob, my friend, had gotten twenty silver dollars from one of the many cashiers and proceeded to start pumping them into the machines at a rapid pace. It seemed like almost immediately the machines started to pay off. This kindled his interest and, before long he asked me to help hold some of his winnings. I cupped my hands together and he quickly filled them both with dollar coins. When he had used about half of them, it happened! He hit the jackpot, and silver dollars started flowing out of the machine like water. "Here," he shouted, "help me with these." He was stuffing his pockets as quickly as he could. Some of the dollars fell to the floor and started rolling around. By now, everyone was watching, and many laughing at our pleasant plight. I started stuffing the pockets of the Cravenette with dollars and they soon became full. (They were very large pockets.) The weight pulling on my shoulders made it difficult to walk. I expected the coat to tear at any moment. Finally, the machine stopped spitting coins. An attendant came over with a basket to help us after we had filled all of our pockets. I learned, later, that one of the major entertainments at the Club was to watch a "Jackpot winner" attempt to catch and carry all of his winnings. It always provided a laugh for the onlookers.

Somehow we managed to make our way to one of the cashier booths. We cashed in most of the silver for paper. The pockets of my clothes were all stretched out of shape and I thought the Cravenette was a goner. The next day I sent all the clothes to the cleaners. Apparently they knew what they were doing, for when the clothes came back, they were all pressed into shape and looked almost like new again.

I never forgot the occasion, and I kept the Cravenette hanging in my closet from that time on, over sixty years. [When Dad passed away, we disposed of all of his clothes which could be used to advantage by someone else. The Cravenette is still hanging in a corner of one of Mom's closet. An occasional glimpse brings back many found memories of Dad for her also.]

When the time for me to show up at the wedding arrived, I felt I was dressed to fill the part as a social reporter for a major newspaper. Although I was nervous at the time, I enjoyed hob-knobbing with the wealthy and was impressed with all the attention they gave me which I hadn't at all expected. I had a very nice time and was pleased to write an elaborate story relating the affair. Naturally, the editor cut it about in half, and would have cut it even more if it had not been for the fact that the bride's & groom's families were friends of the newspaper owners and were expecting a very elaborate spread in our paper. When the story came out in the paper, the social editor came to me and told me that word had come back to him, through the owners of the paper, of what a wonderful impression the young reporter from the *Enquirer* had made. He told me not to let it all go to my head. Even though I had made a good impression, the regular social reporter, once again, took over and it was quite a while before I received another social assignment. I found out later that the regular social reporter had ties in high places, and he was not interested in being up-staged by any young "junior" reporter.

Before long, a need for reporters to cover police stories developed. Once again it seemed I got the job by default. Stories were developing, and I was the only one available at the time to cover them. As my written stories began to gain favor with the editors, I started to receive more and more outside assignments. Soon I was assigned my own police precinct to cover. I was to become a full time street reporter. The police precinct to which I was assigned was in the roughest part of town. When the police cars would role, I would jump in beside the policemen or would ride on the running-boards of the open touring cars, holding onto my hat as my coat tails flapped in the breeze. On other occasions I would ride on the firetrucks or the ambulances (a sign of things to come).

My first murders and shootings were a little hard to take. Although I had managed to see a good bit of life in my first twenty years, there were sights I encountered as a reporter which made my stomach do flips and my heart pound wildly. Many times I would wind up covered with blood of the victims and my clothes would have to go to the cleaners the next day.

Fortunately, I do not recall many of the details of the variously gory incidents, but I do recall one incident which gave us all a good number of laughs when we looked back on it.

It was late one summer night when we had received a call to come to a domestic fight which had broken out in one of the rougher neighborhoods in our already rough precinct.

It had rained earlier, and the streets were slick and shining. This night I had managed to find a seat in the back of one of the Model T patrol cars. We were roaring along through the city streets, with the siren wailing as loud as it would go. There had been a report of someone brandishing a butcher knife at the site of the squabble, and it was felt it would be best if we could get on the scene as quickly as possible to try to avoid some very unfortunate (and messy) police work.

Suddenly, as we crossed over the trolley tracts at a very irregular street intersection, we heard a very loud thump, and the Model T came to a quick, grinding stop. We all jumped out to see what we had hit or run over. As we looked underneath the car we started to laugh. Somehow the engine in the car had come loose. When we hit the bump, it shook loose and literally fell under the car. What a predicament! Needless to say, we never did get to the scene of the fracas. The other cars in our group did. As we heard later, we were fortunate in not making it. The affair turned into a real melee, and became unusually bloody. I had missed a first hand witness of a good story. I was glad to be able to report the testimony of those who had made it to the scene rather than to have been there myself.

Each day or night after the paper was put to bed, I would walk home, a distance of four miles or more to Dayton. If the weather was bad, or I was tired after a busy work session, I would ride home on the trolley.

One morning, after I had spent the night working at the paper, I was kind of tired and I decided to take the trolley home. It was about 4:00 AM when I stepped off the trolley car in Dayton at the corner of Sixth Street and Berry Street. It was just a short walk from there to the old C & O Railroad station. Behind the station was a huge hill known as Perry's Hill. It was a bright, sunny morning and the sky was already well lit. I heard a strange noise and just happened to look up to the top of the hill. There, hanging just a few feet above the ground was a huge dirigible. I was quite shocked to see it hovering there, so close to the ground.

As I stood watching, a rope ladder dropped out of the gondola and a man started to climb down. When the passenger reached the ground and disembarked, the dirigible slowly rose into the air and left on its voyage. I was anxious to find out who the man was and to find out how he arranged this unusual method of delivery, so I waited for him at the bottom of the hill. I watched him walking down a path which was carved in the face of the hill. Not wanting to appear overly aggressive, I waited at the side of the railroad station with the thought that this was his destination. I was fooled, however when he was met on the other side of the station by a "Cincy" taxi-cab. Before I could get to the taxi he had entered and was gone on his way.

When I got home I told everyone of my strange encounter. We all spent the balance of the day wondering and contemplating what was the meaning of my unusual encounter. Later that night, when I went to work at the paper and told of my unusual experience, one of the older reporters was able to enlighten me as to what I had observed. He advised me that the person I had seen was a Commander Rosendahl, the pilot of one of the major airships. His home was in Ohio, not too far from Cincinnati. On occasions, usually early in the morning, he would take advantage of uncrowded conditions and make an unscheduled stop in Dayton in an effort to facilitate a visit to his home.

The time was in the early '20s. It was not uncommon to see other large dirigibles passing over our home. Some of the names I remember of the other airships were the *Akron*, *Los Angeles*, *Macon* and *Shenandoah*. These were some of the largest in the world, with the exception of the German built airships.

Working at the newspaper had many advantages. One of them was being able to find out what was happening in your backyard as well as what was happening in the rest of the world.

In the ensuing years, I learned that my pay boost which I had received was still only a part of what I needed to keep going. Although there had been other raises beyond the initial ten dollars, it was still not as much as I needed. I stuck it out for several years, because the work was exciting and really had the promise of good things to come. Finally, I became impatient and decided it was about time for me to stop sponging on my family and to do something which would provide a better income. I had reached a point on the paper where I had to wait for someone to die or retire before I would be promoted. At the time, that seemed to be an insurmountable and unbearably long time. My sisters, Lill and Ester, were helpful by feeding me and giving me a place to live near my work. My mother [Elizabeth (née Bareswelt) Frotscher], sister Elisabeth, and brother Carl were living on the farm which was 30 miles away. In those days finding dependable transportation to make that trip everyday was extremely difficult and expensive. So I again started looking for another way to expand my horizons.

*   *   *

In early July 1929, Bud, Mary, and Bud's mother, Elizabeth, returned to Kentucky where Bud and Mary were married in the town of Newport. The newlyweds then moved into a rented house on Passaic Street in the town of Maywood, about four miles northwest of Little Ferry. In 1947, they purchased their own home at 153 Fairmont Avenue in the same town.[187]

Fig. IV-32. Mary and Bud Frotscher ca. 1929.

While living in Maywood, Bud held various positions in the maintenance shop of the Public Service Coordinated Transport Company. He worked there for over thirty years, retiring in 1965. He also was very active in civic services. Bud was responsible for the formation and operation of the Maywood First Aid and Emergency Squad and served as one of its first lieutenants and its second captain. He also gave of his time to the Boy Scouts of America. He served as a committeeman for Troop No. 77 and a merit badge councilor. (The author recalls receiving his First Aid Merit Badge, thanks to his Uncle Bud.)

On 12 January 1934, their only child was born: William Franklin Frotscher, Junior. Mary then took a leave of absence from her profession for about five years to care for her young son. However, during World War II, when son Billy was six or seven, Mary returned to nursing at the Hackensack

Hospital. This was done to avoid possible separation from her family. During this period, the U.S. Government was drafting unemployed registered nurses for the war effort.

Fig. IV-33. Frotscher family home at 153 Fairmont Avenue, Maywood, NJ. (Photo taken 02 May 1997.)

Fig. IV-34. Mary (née Rucker) Frotscher circa 1945

In order to continue to be home for her son during the day, Mary worked the 11 PM to 7 AM shift. She did this until her retirement in January 1969. Soon after that, Mary and Bud relocated to Newburg, Pennsylvania to be near the home of their son and his young family.

Bud passed away on 27 January 1990 at the Chambersburg Hospital in Chambersburg, Pennsylvania. The cause of death was colon cancer. His remains were cremated. Mary, now in her nineties, continues a very active life in the Frotscher family home in Newburg, a few hundred yards from her son.

Frances (née Rucker) Skelton (1908-   )

Frances Rucker learned clerical skills at Hackensack High School. In 1923, she and several classmates applied for a clerical job at an employment agency in New York City. The only jobs available at the time were in the area of lower Manhattan. The commute from Little Ferry was tedious. It began with a walk to the Ridgefield Park Railroad Station, followed by a ride on the New York Central Railroad to the ferry docks at Weehawken. Many of the ferry boats went directly across the Hudson River to 42nd Street, a ride that would take about ten minutes. However, the Cortland Street ferry went from Weehawken to downtown Manhattan; a ride took about thirty minutes. This was followed by another fifteen minute walk. A one-way trip took a little less than two hours. Frances recalls that if she left home before 7:15 AM, she was usually in the office before 9:00.

Her first job was with Page Treadway and Company on Chambers Street mailing out samples of various paper products. Frances worked there only a short time before her next position at an insurance company on Maiden Lane, one block from Wall Street. (Because there already were two other women there with the same forename, Frances was called "Fay.") It was during this period that Frances also was honing her thespian skills. In January 1927 she starred in the Bohemian show entitled *No. 27 Boulevard* playing the role of Josephine.[188]

Fig. IV-35. Frances Rucker at about 18 years of age.

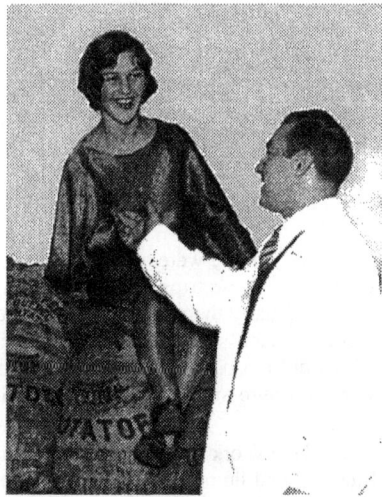

Fig. IV-36. Frances Rucker posing for a calendar for the Howard Smith and Company. (The photo was taken on 08 October 1929, twenty-one days before the crash of the stock market.)

"Fay" and several of her co-workers left the insurance company to protest the poor working conditions. Her next position was with a claim bureau on West Street, still in lower Manhattan, but near the Hudson River. This company was involved in filing claims due to loss or damage against the railroads hauling fruits and vegetables. Frances' position there lasted until a short time after 29 October 1929 — the crash of the stock market and the start of the great American Depression. Because she was the last one hired, Frances was the first let go. As luck would have it, another agency, Atlantic Commission, a subsidiary of the Atlantic and Pacific Tea Company,[189] located only three blocks away, was looking for a good secretary. Because of her previous job performance, Frances had an excellent recommendation from her former employer and was hired immediately.

In 1927, Floyd Skelton, known to family and friends as "Babe," because he was the last of seven children born to Isaac Franklin Skelton and Augusta (née Dieterle) Skelton, came east from Kentucky. He journeyed with his boyhood friend, Bud Frotscher. Bud and Babe made the trip on motorcycles to visit Bud's mother, Elizabeth (née Bareswelt) Frotscher. Elizabeth was renting an apartment in the house adjacent to the Rucker home on Washington Avenue in Little Ferry to care for her sick daughter. In the years to come, Bud and Babe would marry the Rucker sisters, Mary and Frances, respectively.

Details of the motorcycle trip from Kentucky to New Jersey are well told in the memoirs of Bud Frotscher. The following is another chapter from the book *Dad's Stories*:[190]

CHAPTER 18

THE MOTORCYCLE TRIP

Actually, there were a number of motorcycle trips which we made around the midwest area. These trips were excursions, when free time would allow us the luxury of a lark. Usually there would be a number of us that would get together and ride off as sort of a "Hell's Angels" group. Our friends, for the most part, had limited incomes which did not permit all the fancy trimmings as the California group had, but we were an impressive bunch to meet on the road in our own unique way.

The New York trip was quite different from the others. It came at a time when our finances had bottomed out. (Almost everything we had went into paying bills accumulated at the "Bus Inn.") The basic reason for the trip wasn't a lark, as the others had been. This, instead, was a journey to find work in an effort to re-establish ourselves as a productive part of society.

There was an air of dire need about this trip and it probably never would have been made if it weren't for those circumstances. Our poor financial situation drove us to set out on the journey in a very sorry state. Neither of our motorcycles were in good mechanical condition. They were running however, and since Babe and I had reasonable mechanical ability, we felt if something should give out, we would just repair it on the spot. This is what we usually did when on the road, anyway.

The other problem which we had could not be so easily corrected. When we left on the trip, five dollars was all the money we could scrape together. Surprisingly enough, this would have been enough money to make the trip in those days, as long as there were no major problems or expenses. We planned to sleep alongside the road when we had to sleep at all, and we felt we could manage to scrounge up enough food to keep us alive until we got to my family's home in Little Ferry, N.J. Our other major plan was to cope with whatever might happen, when it happened. This really wasn't any plan at all, but many things seem to get done this way, even when the situation appears to be impossible. It was with this line of thinking that we packed a few of our meager possessions and started on our odyssey.

It didn't take very long for our contingency plan to be challenged. About 25 miles from Cincy, on our way to Hamilton, Ohio, the brake arm broke on Babe's bike. Fortunately, I had relatives in Hamilton so we headed for their house. The bike would still run. The major problem occurred when Babe would try to stop. He would have to slow down using engine compression. Unfortunately his well-worn motorcycle no longer had very much compression. This tended to complicate things a bit more.

I had several relatives who lived in Hamilton. The closest to where we were, at the time, was my Aunt's house. When we arrived there it was just getting dark. They were quite surprised, but happy to see us (at least they made us feel that way). The first thing they did was give us a big meal which was very well received. After visiting awhile, they arranged a place for us to sleep.

So far, our contingency plan was working well. On our first night of the journey, we went to bed with full stomachs and spent the night sleeping in warm, comfortable beds. The next morning after having a whopping big breakfast, Johnny, my cousin, took Babe and me over to my brother Herman's house which was not very far away.

Herman, my oldest brother, was very much amused to see us and hear of our plight. He was a good bit older than I was,— actually, old enough to be my father. Although there was such a major difference in our age, we got along quite well most of the time. He felt it was his job to take me under his wing and teach me many of the things which he knew. I guess he realized that with my Dad away working most of the time, I needed some fatherly instruction and help. He filled in whenever he could. Here was another opportunity for him to help out. Within a very short time he had the brake arm welded and rebuilt to better than new. He took us to our motorcycles. Before long we had the refurbished part back on the bike in working order. He laughingly slapped us both on the back and sent us on our way.

As we started off on the next leg of our journey we felt very confident. We had survived a major catastrophe and managed to come out on top. We still had the five dollars in our pockets, our bellies were full, and we had a wonderful night's rest. Our exuberant feelings didn't last long, however. As we neared Dayton, Ohio, an exhaust port plug came off Babes bike and rolled off the road into some tall grass.

As in the previous breakdown, the motorcycle still ran well. The biggest problem was the ear-splitting noise it made. The other problem was that Babe had to be very careful not to have his pants set on fire from the hot exhaust blowing out of the engine near his leg.

We must have spent an hour or more searching through the grass for the old plug. It was not to be found, however. In frustration, we gave up the search and started down the road again, really not knowing how we were going to deal with this situation. Although we were still mobile, it wasn't at all comfortable to continue traveling in this way. Besides, we were aware the noise would probably cause us to be stopped when we got to a town. Even then, people were very much aware of noise pollution caused by motor vehicles. In fact, one of the major objections people had to them was all the racquet they made, as compared to horse-drawn transportation. Laws were quickly drafted to curb engine noise, and these laws were strictly enforced.

Luck was still on our side. Someone was definitely looking out for us. A short way down the road we came across an Indian motorcycle service shop. We explained our circumstances to the owner of the shop who listened intently and, apparently, with great compassion. He instructed his mechanics to fix us up and get us back on the road. The mechanic located a used exhaust plug which was laying around the shop from a junked engine. He put it in Babe's motorcycle and it did the job as good as new. When we offered to pay, the owner pointed down the road, and told us to get going before the repair job would wind up costing much more than we could afford. We thanked him prolifically, knowing full well we couldn't afford to pay him much of anything, and quickly obeyed his instruction before he decided to change his mind about our bill. Fortune was still with us.

Our motorcycles, though rather old and dilapidated, were easy on gas and oil. After spending most of the day driving across Ohio, we arrived at Wheeling, West Virginia, just as darkness was beginning to set in. Two problems set upon us about the same time. By this time we were very low on gas. The long day's ride had been quite tiring, especially coupled with the stress involved with the exhaust plug situation in Dayton. We had spent about a dollar of our funds on some lunch.

The original plan of sleeping beside the road no longer seemed as acceptable as it had before we left. In our preliminary plans, we pictured spending the night under the stars in a thick grass lined pasture. Under those circumstances throwing down a blanket or canvass tarp would have been quite delightful. Now, in reality, things were not quite so ideal. The sky looked like we were in for a good storm about any minute. Also, there were no thick grass lined pastures along side the road. Instead, there were factories, steel mills, hard sidewalks, and, everywhere else shoulder-to-shoulder tenement type houses. Hardly any of these had grass lawns in front of them.

It was easy to see we were going to have to change our plans. We started searching for a cheap bed in a low cost hotel or, possibly, a boarding house. The least expensive and reasonable place we could find cost about $2 for each of us. We also were faced with the fact that we had to provide for the safe-keeping of our motorcycles. Even though they were not high priced items, they were all that we had to depend on to take us on the trip. We were sure that some of the young men in Wheeling would be very anxious to take our bikes for a joy ride once we left them un-attended.

Fortunately, I had several brothers, and being the youngest they all kind of looked after me. My brother, Henry, was living in Little Ferry, N.J. also. We counted on him to rescue us from the latest situation.

There was a Western Union telegraph office near the place where we had decided to spend the night. We quickly rode over to the office just in time to catch the lady who ran the office getting ready to close for the evening. We told her of our plight, and she, too had compassion for us, and agreed to stay open long enough for us to wire my brother, Henry, and have him send us enough money to complete our journey. I believe the poor lady wound up getting into much more than she had bargained for.

Although she quickly got the message off to my brother requesting the financial help, she did not realize the additional time which was required for the message to be delivered to my brother. It was then necessary for Henry to find a telegraph office which was still open and go there to give them the cash. The Hackensack, N.J. office was the closest. It was about a half hour's drive away from his house. Henry first enlisted the help of my other brother, Carl, who was also staying in Little Ferry at this time. They both pooled their funds to come up with the $20 we had requested. Together, they went off to the telegraph office in order to send the money on its way.

It was after midnight before the money finally arrived in Wheeling. By this time both Babe and I, and also the telegraph operator were all very tired. Her husband and son had come looking for her, wondering why she hadn't come home from work at her usual time. It was obvious they were very much annoyed with the inconvenience and interruptions we had caused in their lives. As the night wore on, we became very much aware of the sleep they were all losing on our behalf. When the money did finally come through, Babe and I thanked them profusely for their helping us out. They nodded their heads and mumbled something to the effect of "How happy they all were to be able to help out." As we drove away from the Western Union office, Babe and I decided our contingency plans, though working well for us, were not real helpful to our friends, relatives, and many of the people we encountered along the way.

We left Wheeling early in the morning in hopes of completing the trip before we had to spend more money on overnight accommodations and a safe parking space for our bikes. Late in the afternoon we arrived in Baltimore. It didn't take much effort to get lost. As we were blundering along, a motorcycle policeman pulled up alongside us with his red lights flashing. He signaled to pull over. In a way we were glad to see him, for we needed directions, but we were a bit apprehensive as to why he had decided to pull us over. We soon found out.

Somewhere along the road between Wheeling and Baltimore the license plate had fallen off my motorcycle. I was fortunate to have the owner's papers along so I showed them to the police office. He was quite amazed to find out we were from Kentucky. After he had heard our plans for traveling to New Jersey; he smiled and just shook his head in disbelief. He next told us that he really should stay with us for awhile in order that no one else would stop us and give us a rough time. He also said, "As long as you don't get into trouble for anything else, you will probably be all right." He was correct. We watched our "P's and Q's" until we were far out of Baltimore and everything went without further mishap. The other crucial bit of information he gave us before he left us was that we were traveling in the wrong direction and if we really wanted to get to New York, we had better turn around and go the other way. Otherwise, we would soon be back in Wheeling and would have to send another wire to my brother, Henry. This time we were sure the telegraph operator would not be so quick to agree to helping us beyond the realm of her duties.

The next major city along the route (U.S. 40) was Philadelphia. The city was in the midst of a huge celebration. Traffic was thick and horribly congested. It did not take long for us to get lost again. But, once again, the police were quick to come to our aid. At first, we were worried about the lost license plate. However, the police were too busy with traffic problems to show any concern. They got us pointed in the right direction, and soon we were nearing the outskirts of the city limits.

The day was quickly drawing to a close and we hadn't had much to eat. We soon found a pleasant looking diner. It reminded me of our Bus Inn, even though it was much larger and much more elaborate. I was thinking, at the time, maybe, if we could have stuck with it, we might have been able to have a place like this someday. The possibilities didn't seem very far away; but the final word was that we were just not able to swing the financing. That was the key factor when all was said and done.

When we had filled our bellies and again started on our way, we noticed it had started to drizzle while we were in the diner. We talked about trying to find a place to stay for the night. The weather had warmed a good bit and, even though it was damp, it was not very cold. We had the remnants of leather jackets such as most motorcycle riders wear. They were quite worn and ragged, but the leather protected us from the wind, and goggles shielded much of our eyes and upper faces. The other factor which was effecting our decision whether or not to lay over for the night was our concern for the finances. Although we had made the addition to our coffers in Wheeling, the money seemed to be disappearing rather quickly. So we decided that if we could stick with it a few more hours through the night, we could be in Little Ferry by morning.

We tied everything up tight on our motorcycles, zipped up our jackets and pulled our goggles down over our faces. Together we started up the road, first quite cautiously, then as soon as we regained our confidence, at an ever increasing speed.

The rain also seemed to be falling at an ever increasing rate. We had crossed over the Delaware River and soon found ourselves barreling along the famous White Horse Pike, crossing central New Jersey, heading for our destination just outside of New York.

In those days, many of the roads were paved with cobble stones. When the stones were freshly laid they had fairly sharp edges where they had been cut into rectangles, so they would fit closely together to form a reasonably smooth level surface. As the years went by, and traffic increased, the edges of the stones became chipped off, especially by the steel rims used on most horse drawn vehicles. With the advent and increased use of rubber tires on cars and trucks, the edges of the stones became rounded and polished by the rubber. Soon many of the stones developed a very slippery crown surface. When they were wet they became deadly to vehicle travel.

Babe was riding in the lead, and, being a bit more venturesome than I, he was setting a rather fast pace. I started to fall a good distance behind and decided I had better try to keep up before we became separated. As I gunned the engine to catch up, the rear wheel skidded sideways and I had difficulties trying to keep the bike upright.

With much more concern and care I slowly accelerated so that I would not lose traction again. I realized I had better catch up with Babe and caution him of the slippery road surface conditions. Carefully, I eased my bike up alongside and tried to holler to him to slow down. He couldn't hear what I was saying, so I rode past and tried motioning for him to slow down.

Apparently he thought I was trying to race, for he didn't seem to slow at all. Suddenly, there was an unexpected flash from his headlight as it swept from one side of the road to the other. Then it became dark as the light no longer lit the roadway, but was now flashing out across the fields at the side of the road. I realized his bike was down, and both he and the bike were somewhere behind me, sliding along the cobble stones to who knows where.

In an effort to stop to see what had happened, I, too, started to slide. As soon as I touched the brakes, the back wheel took off sideways, and soon the whole bike was down on its side, scraping along the cobble stones which no longer appeared to be very smooth at all. Occasionally, sparks would fly as the paint wore away and bare metal rubbed against the hard stones. I was fortunate enough to get my lower leg out from under the motorcycle and was able to ride out the fall on top of the motorcycle with a minimum of injuries.

We were lucky. There was very little traffic on the road so we were not faced with the immediate danger of being run-over by a passing vehicle. When I finally came to a halt and was able to determine that I was not hurt badly, I called to Babe to see if he was still alive. Surprisingly, he had come to a stop not very far from where I was lying and quickly replied that he, too, had not sustained any serious injuries but that he was bleeding from some scrapes and was a bit sore in a few places.

We looked down the road and noticed a pair of headlights coming in our direction. It didn't take long before we realized we had better get ourselves and our motorcycles off the road before something more serious happened.

Quickly, we picked up our bikes and pushed them to the side of the road. When the oncoming headlights became dangerously close they began to zig-zag back and forth across the road. We realized the car was out of control and wondered if and where we should run to get out of its way.

Just before coming to us, the car left the road and skidded up an embankment and came to an abrupt stop. Babe and I quickly ran over to the car to see if anyone was injured. When we reached the car, we cautiously opened the door. Inside, behind the wheel, sat a lone, elderly man. He was shaking badly and was barely able to speak. Finally, he pulled himself together enough to ask if he had run over those two boys who were lying in the road with their motorcycles. We assured him that we were the two boys, and, except for a few bumps and scrapes, we were in fine shape. After helping him get his car back on the road and calming him down a good bit, we reassured him that it was okay to continue on his journey. Before he left he told us he was a minister for a nearby black congregation, and that he was on his way home after a prayer meeting. He was aware that this stretch of road became slippery when it was wet, but had never experienced anything like he had that night.

The episode with the car and the minister distracted Babe and me from our falls and accompanying bruises. After the minister had driven off, we checked out our motorcycles looking for damages. Except for a little missing paint and a dent or two more than they had before the falls, they were in as good operating condition as they had been when we left Cincinnati. We started them up, and, this time, proceeded a lot more cautiously, at least until we got off the cobble stones.

In a few hours we had reached Jersey City, New Jersey. The rain had stopped, and it was fairly nice traveling in the early morning hours. On the outside of the city we ran into a lot of traffic. By this time people were going to work. At the intersection of Hudson Boulevard we sat and waited for some time for a break in traffic which would allow us to enter. All at once we were surrounded by what seemed to be a posse of motorcycle police. They saw us sitting on our bikes at the intersection and realized the problem we were having. Their first questions were: "Are you lost?" and "Is there anything we can do to help?" The answer to the first question was 'No," even though we really weren't exactly sure where we were. I had traveled through this section on some of my previous trips to New Jersey, but didn't know the area too well.

The answer to the second question was, "Yes, you could get us onto Hudson Boulevard and take us to Dan Kelly's Hill." We would surely be able to find our way from there. The leader of the group smiled and said, "Okay, follow us." With that, he gave a wave of his arm to his group and off we went, pulling right into the middle of traffic, surrounded on all sides by the motorcycle mounted police.

Naturally, the traffic on the boulevard quickly slowed and made plenty of room for our official entourage. From there on we traveled very quickly to our disembarkation point at Dan Kelly's Hill. We really felt honored being escorted by this very important looking group. They had quickly gathered into a formation. We were instructed to ride in the center where we would be well protected from the traffic which steered clear of the uniformed group on their impressive white motorcycles.

When we reached our turn off point, the leader of the group motioned us to the side of the road. He pointed his leather gloved finger in the direction we wanted to travel and said, "If you guys ever get back into this area be sure to look us up. Oh yes, and it would be a good idea if you would get a license plate for that motorcycle. You may not need one in Kentucky, but around here they are rather important." With that we thanked him for their help and they quickly rode off with a loud roar, the leader touching his hand to his hat in an informal salute. When the troop had left, Babe and I looked at each other and both of us beamed with a feeling of importance following our "official" escort.

Within minutes we arrived in Little Ferry and were welcomed with open arms. Everyone was anxious to hear the tales of our recent adventure, and many times, thereafter, we told the stories over and over again.

* * *

Following a protracted courtship, Frances and Floyd were wed on Sunday, 02 August 1931. The exchange of nuptials took place at the Evangelical Congregational Church at the intersection of Main Street and Marshall Avenue in Little Ferry. After the ceremony, a reception was held at the Rucker home on Washington Avenue. The following day, the bride and groom left for Dayton, Kentucky, to honeymoon for two weeks in Floyd's boyhood hometown.

Upon their return to New Jersey, the newlyweds rented a house in Emerson, a small town a few miles north of Hackensack. In his earlier years, Floyd learned about power systems, largely steam engines. This learning came from his father, Isaac Franklin Skelton. Isaac spent his early life on the Ohio River, working around steam engines. He worked his way up on the river boats from deck hand, to mate, to engineer, and finally, to captain. In 1895, he received his Masters License.[191]

Following in his father's footsteps, Floyd also spent most of his years around mechanical power systems. His first job in New Jersey was at the Continental Paper Company in Bogota, a town northeast of Little Ferry. Unfortunately Floyd's general state of health was not good. Because of severe stomach problems, he was unable to sleep well at night and regretfully, he was found sleeping on the job at the paper mill and discharged.

The couple was living, in part, on money Frances had saved during the years before she was married — but that was running out. Unable to find work because of the depression, in December of 1931, Floyd returned to his parents' home in Kentucky and Frances moved back in with her family in Little Ferry. Fortunately, she had not quit her job in New York City — one which paid $25 for a 5-$1/2$ day-week. (It was half-day on Saturdays, from 9 until noon.) Most of those earnings went to the support of the Rucker household. Neither of her brothers, Eddie and Bep, were working and her father's butcher shop was not making money. Actually Adolf was doing a good business, but people were unable to pay, largely because of the depression.

Four months later, on April third, the day before Frances' twenty-fourth birthday, Floyd returned to his bride in New Jersey with a birthday present, a bathrobe. (Frances recalls that the gift was purchased with winnings from either a pinochle or poker game.) For the next four years, Floyd and Frances lived in the Rucker family home at 135 Washington Avenue. During this time, Floyd turned the back yard at the Rucker household into a very prolific vegetable garden. Not long after his return, he was hired by Edward Klemmer as a stationery engineer at Spencer Kellogg and Sons, Incorporated of Edgewater, New Jersey — a position he held until his retirement in 1967 — at the age of 62.

Fig. IV-37. Frances (née Rucker) and Floyd Skelton
taken at the Rucker home in Little Ferry following
their wedding on 02 August 1931.

As mentioned before, Floyd's health was not good. Throughout his life, he seemed to go from one serious ailment to another. The first serious incident occurred in 1937 when his appendix ruptured. Frances received an emergency phone call at work from her sister, Mary, telling her that Floyd had been rushed to the Hackensack Hospital for an emergency operation. While on the operating table, it was discovered that gangrene had already set in. This incident had other negative repercussions: At the time, because of the depression and difficulty in finding work, married women were not expected to work, the idea being that they would be taking the job away from a man. It was not known in Frances' office that she was a married woman. Because the company telephone operator listened in on the emergency phone call, that secret was out. Fortunately, because of her excellent performance record, the decision of upper management was to ignore the facts and continue under the guise that she was still "Miss Frances Rucker."

Eventually, Floyd and Frances vacated the Rucker household and moved into their own apartment in Ridgefield Park. Several years later they purchased their first home in Teaneck, a town immediately north of Bogota.[192] Except for a fifteen year hiatus rearing her son, Frances (née Rucker) Skelton spent most of her life in one office or another. She continued working in the Wall Street area of New York City until she had to quit for maternity reasons.

Fig. IV-38. Skelton Family home at 682 Kent Avenue, Teaneck, New Jersey.
(Photo taken in 1941.)

When her son was in his early teens, Frances returned to the work place. She first worked as a bookkeeper at the First National Bank in Hackensack; then for a short time, as a secretary at the Hackensack Court House. In 1962, she began working in the Physics Department at Fairleigh Dickinson University (FDU) in Teaneck. This job was a delight: The University was only a seven minute walk from her home, the daily activities were very interesting, rarely the "same ol' thing," and she was very well liked by faculty and students alike. She advanced to the position of Office Manager and soon was running the business end of the FDU Physics Department single-handedly. Frances continued there until her retirement in 1971, at the age of 63. Following that she and Floyd left their home in Teaneck and purchased a house in Shippensburg, Pennsylvania, near the Frotschers.

Fig. IV-39. Frances impersonating Elvis Presley singing *Jail House Rock* at the Shippensburg Senior Citizens Center competition. (The performance took first prize.)

Frances Skelton to vie for Ms. Senior America title

Frances Skelton, representing the Shippensburg Senior Center, will vie for the 1989 Ms. Pennsylvania Senior America crown, Oct. 16-19. The pageant will be held at the Genetti Dinner Playhouse and Conference Center in Hazleton.

The winner of the pageant will represent Pennsylvania in the Ms. Senior America Pageant in April 1990.

Each contestant is judged on personal interview, a three-minute talent section, a philosophy of life, and appearance in an evening gown.

Frances is being sponsored by the senior citizens of the Shippensburg center.

Frances Skelton

Fig. IV-40. Item from the *News Chronicle* Shippensburg, PA, 07 July 1989.

Floyd's poor state of health plagued him throughout much of his life. One factor contributing to this was the fact that he became addicted to tobacco at the age of fourteen. He was never able to quit and passed away in 1982 at the age of 78. He died with cancer in his right lung and bones. His final years were not pleasant.

Frances continues to lead a very active life. In 1989, she won third place in the competition for Ms. Senior Pennsylvania, having been selected by the Shippensburg Senior Citizens Center to represent their group. This selection was undoubtedly based in part on her vibrant, bubbly personality. Throughout life, Frances has never been at a loss for words and is often the life of the party. She continues to be very active in the Senior Citizens Center, serving as their secretary for many years, and first place winner at many of their competitive events.

In 1995, Frances served as principal editor of a book entitled *Ike, This Is You*. The work is co-authored by her son and Isaac Newton Skelton-III, a third cousin of her husband. In appreciation for her efforts, U.S. Congressman Isaac Newton Skelton-IV hosted Fran, her son, and grandson, Isaac Patton Skelton, to lunch in the U.S. Capitol.

Fig. IV-41. Congressman Ike Skelton, Earl Skelton, and Frances Skelton at the Rayburn House Office Building, U.S. Capitol in 1995.

Edward Rucker (1909-___)

During World War II, both Rucker sons were called into service. Edward fought in the European theater from Normandy until the collapse of Third Reich in the spring of 1945 and his younger brother, Adolph[193] was sent to the Pacific theater of operations and served there until the latter part of 1945.

Following his induction into the Army on 12 February 1943,[194] Eddie received his basic training at Camp Hulen in Texas.[195] It was there that he was assigned to Able Battery in the 473rd Anti-Aircraft Artillery Battalion. On 14 April 1943, Private Rucker qualified as a Sharpshooter with the M1 30 caliber rifle.[196] The role of anti-aircraft units was large defensive against enemy air attack on fixed ground installations, such as staging areas, rail heads, and field artillery units. Their primary weapon was an anti-aircraft gun mounted on an armored truck with front tires and a rear tractor drive. These were commonly known as "half-tracks."

On 06 February 1944, the 473rd was transferred to Camp Polk in Louisiana for additional training. Less than a month later, on 03 March, the outfit was ordered to Camp Claiborne and from there on 26 March, to Camp Kilmer in New Jersey — their "POE" (Point of Embarkation). On Friday, 07 April 1944, the more than 800 members of the 473rd Anti-Aircraft Battalion sailed aboard the S.S. *Ile de France* bound for Liverpool, England. *D-Day was less than two months away.*

Fig. IV-42. Review of Able Battery, 473rd Anti-Aircraft Artillery Battalion, somewhere in Europe, 1944-45.

The unit spent the last days of April and all of May in England. For a time they were assigned to western air defense of England. Fortunately, Eddie's outfit was not to be among the first to go ashore at Normandy on D-Day. On 18 June, the battalion was ordered to protect the advanced fighter bases in the vicinity of Ashford in Kent. Here they spent several weeks combating the German V-1 rockets, the so-called "Buzz-Bombs." It was not until 10 July, that the 473rd landed in France. This was on Utah Beach in Normandy. About a week later, they came under enemy artillery fire for the first time — eight men in C Battery were wounded.

Fig. IV-43. Staff Sergeant Edward Rucker, U.S. Army, taken in early 1944 before his embarkation for Europe.

On 20 July, squads from the outfit were attached to three infantry regiments. Their orders were to force gaps through the hedgerows, natural defensive barriers the Germans were using to impede the Allied breakout from the Cherbourg Peninsula. "Our particular task was to spray these hedgerows until the infantrymen could get close enough to close in. It was rough going because we often had to expose ourselves to get into firing position. Our [half-] tracks became the target for every Kraut that could fire a gun. We were lucky in a way, for in that holocaust of mortar shells and machine gun fire, we only left one man."[197]

Following the outbreak from the hedgerow country, the 473rd was transferred from the First Army to the Third Army, then under the command of the renown General George S. Patton. They fought their way across northern France, into Belgium, and then into Holland. During the Battle of the Bulge in late December, they were stationed in the Dutch towns of Schaesberg, Eygelshoven, and Niewenhagen. Actions in the Rhineland led to crossing the Roer River on 28 February and, within a month the last natural obstacle before Germany — the Rhine.

"On April 11th, orders were received to withdraw from our sector and proceed to aid the 2nd Armored. That meant back to the main attack front to our fast driving, hard hitting role once more. But we found that the same punch was not needed. Something was happening — inside the 'Fatherland'. The German armies which had been drawn in to defend it were suffering their worst defeat. The Third Reich was getting groggy; this was the last round. Air activity on the enemy's part, falling off sharply, had by now almost ceased to exist. Herman Goering didn't have enough gasoline left for his cigarette lighter. The war was lost and the supermen were beginning to realize it. Those leaders who set out to rule Germany for a thousand years and conquer the freedom-loving peoples of the world, were floundering in the pulverized rubble of their own capitol. The beginning of the end was at hand."[198] V-E Day came on 07 May 1945.

It was during a German air attack in France that Technical Staff Sergeant Edward Rucker earned the Purple Heart. He, along with two buddies, went diving for a fox hole when the bombing attack began. Unbeknownst to him at the time, the man on top of him had been killed. Eddie was wounded in the leg by shrapnel. He also was awarded the Good Conduct Medal and was honorably discharged on 19 October 1945[199] at Fort Dix, New Jersey.

Adolph Rucker (1910-   )

The forename of the younger son of Adolf and Matylda (née Prihoda) Rucker was originally "Adolf." In the 1920 census, he is listed as "Otto" and at one time was called "Roy" by friends. But to the family, he has always been known as "Bep." During World War II, the spelling was changed to "Adolph," to distinguish it from Hitler's forename.[200] (In this work, he is referred to formally as <u>Adolph</u> Rucker and informally as <u>Bep</u> Rucker.)

Bep was called into service in 1942. Following a year of training in the states, in the fall of 1943, he sailed on a troop ship west from California. With stopovers at Tasmania and Perth, Australia, he arrived at Bombay, India, thirty-three days later. From there he boarded a troop train for Gaya, in the northeastern Indian province of Bihar. Here Private Rucker began a two year service in the China-Burma-India Theater as part of the maintenance crew of the 459th Fighter Squadron, attached to the U.S. Army Air Corps' 33rd Fighter Group.[201]

Fig. IV-44. Men of the 459th Fighter Squadron; 33rd Fighter Group in Asia circa 1945. Pvt. Adolph Rucker is in the front row, second from the left.

The 459th Fighter Squadron was formed on 01 November 1943 in Eastern Bengal from portions of the then existing 80th Fighter Group, 311th Fighter Bomber Group, and new operational training units from the States. The unit included men from all walks of life and from forty-three different States and several U.S. territories. A major difference between the 459th and other fighter groups was their principal aircraft: the P-38 fighter, known as the "Lightening." The unique twin fuselage of the aircraft supported separate, twin engines. This led the men of the outfit to adopt the squadron insignia of "The Twin Dragons."

Fig. IV-45. Twin Dragon Insignia of
the 459th Fighter Squadron.

The combat missions of the
459th varied from escorting bomber
formations, dive-bombing Japanese
lines of communication and supply,
and air-ground support. Other
activities involved ferrying
munitions and other war materials
over "The Hump" — the
Himalayan Mountains. According
to General Howard Davidson,
Commanding General of the Tenth
Air Force, the success of the 459th
squadron was due in part to "...the
excellent maintenance throughout
the course which resulted in no
flying time being lost through
unserviceability."

Fig. IV-46. Pvt. Adolph "Bep"
Rucker circa 1944 in Asia in front of a
P-38 named *Frances Rebel*.

In early March 1944, the squadron's base of operations was moved to
Chittagon, on the Bay of Bengal — about fifty miles from the Burmese border.
It was there that Bep contracted malaria. He was transferred to a rest and recovery
camp and later returned to his unit.

In January 1945, as the Japanese retreated, the unit moved once again —
this time to Rumkhapalong, on the India-Burma border. From here the 459th
joined in the campaign to drive the Japanese from Burma. At this point of the
war in southeast Asia, the Japanese Air Force was no longer a threat. Thus, the

combat activities of the pilots were largely bombing, bridge destruction, and general ground support.

The high level of success attained by the 459th Fighter Squadron during the war is credited, in part, to "...the superior record of maintenance consistently maintained in the face of adverse conditions..." Sometime after V-J Day, Bep and his service buddies boarded a train bound for Calcutta. From there, he sailed to Ceylon, then through the Suez Canal and Straits of Gibraltar, at last arriving at the Port of New York. He then went from Camp Kilmer to Fort Dix, New Jersey, where he was honorably discharged from the Army. He arrived at the family home in Little Ferry in time for Thanksgiving Dinner 1945. And, by sailing across the Pacific to Asia in 1943 and returning home at the end of the war from the east, Bep became the first member of the family to circumnavigate the globe.

Today, both Eddie and Bep are retired and continue to live at the family home at 135 Washington Avenue in Little Ferry. One of their pastime activities is the raising of show pigeons. Bep has won many awards for his birds.

Fig. IV-47. Pvt. Adolph "Bep" Rucker circa 1943.

Eighth Generation

Joseph Masek (1922 -   )

Joseph {Josef} Masek was born on 10 May 1922 in Prague.[202] He grew up there, working at times in the family restaurant. The Masek family had been in the restaurant business in Prague. A sketch of the family home and restaurant is reproduced below. The original building, erected in 926, is now three stories below ground.

Fig. IV-48. Masek home and restaurant in Prague.

During World War II, Joseph worked as the maître d' on a train that traveled in Nazi occupied western Europe from Stuttgart to Strasbourg. He said he was fortunate to have learned many "tricks of the trade" from his maternal grandfather, Jan Prihoda. Some of these proved very helpful. In early 1945, Joseph was arrested by the Gestapo in Stuttgart for smuggling French prisoners of war out of Germany. As the maître d', young Joseph had control of the rail car. He unknowingly became involved with General Charles DeGaulle's

Marquis Underground Movement. His role was to hide the POWs in the storage bunkers under the dining cars. Before he was caught, he was making two trips a day, crossing the Rhine River each time.

Joseph later immigrated to Canada and there, in Montreal, married Jeanne Nadeau, a woman of French Canadian ancestry. They had a son, Jan Masek, and soon after, Jeanne abandoned the family. Jan was raised by his mother's sister. Some time later, Joseph married again. His new bride was Micheline Marie-Anna Mallet, the daughter of Omer George Mallet, a shipbuilder from Centre St. Simon, New Brunswick, Canada, and Marie-Anna LeBouthilier, his wife. Joseph and Michelle removed to California and there raised two children, Barbara and Marc.

Joseph and Michelle chose Saratoga in Santa Clara County, California as their new home. They opened a very elegant restaurant there, *la Mère Michelle.* It continues in operation today[203] and recently received a glowing review in the *San Jose Mercury News*:

"A perfect 4-star feast in Saratoga ... where diners continue to experience the pleasures of classic four-star dining. The interior is a sumptuous picture of quiet elegance. Handsome furnishings promise comfort without blinding the eye with gaudy fashion. ... All components of the four-star experience are firmly in place at La Mère Michelle."[204]

Fig. IV-49. Front cover of the menu from *la Mère Michelle.*
The ladies are Michelle (née Mallet) Masek (left) and Barbara (née Masek) Henley.
The standing gentlemen are Kenneth Henley, Barbara's husband, and Joseph Masek.

Rudolph Arthur Komarek (1928-   )

To say that Rudy is the most colorful family member of his generation, may be something of an understatement. Here is an excerpt from an article written about him in 1984:[205]

> "His speech began slurring and he was developing breathing problems. Bob said that the only additional information was that he was fifty-ish and his first name was Rudy. 'The Cobra King?' I asked. Bob answered, 'That's my bet.' ... He had arrived unconscious and totally paralyzed. A respirator was keeping him alive.
>
> ... His case will make medical history. ... My visit with Rudy at the Jacobi Hospital was not my first encounter with 'The Cobra King' — nor I suspect my last. Five years ago I saw him in Allenwood Federal Prison."

Rudolph and Carrie (née Rucker) Komarek were parents to two sons, Rudolph Arthur and Robert Edwin. Both were born while their parents lived in the Komarek family home at 62 Marshall Avenue in Little Ferry. [See map in Fig. IV-11.]

Rudolph Arthur Komarek, or "Sonny," or "Rudy," as he is most commonly called, was born on 11 November 1928. When he was eight years old, during a walk with his mother and the family pet dog, "Smoky," Rudy caught his first snake. It was a small, harmless garter snake, but that event marked the beginning of a life long obsession.

Fig. IV-50. Robert Komarek, Billy Frotscher,
and Rudy Komarek taken circa 1940.

During his early years, the family would often take day trips to Bear Mountain State Park, just north of the New York-New Jersey border. Rudy viewed these family outings as hunting opportunities. Catching not only snakes, but unusual turtles and frogs and other inhabitants of the park. Through the years, he sometimes shocked, but often entertained family members and others with his live reptile collection. His cousin, Bill Frotscher, has vivid recollections of feeding time at "Rudy's zoo."[206]

Fig. IV-51. Rudy Komarek and his mother, Carrie (née Rucker) Komarek in 1953.

This passion for collecting living reptiles, especially snakes, turned into a compulsion. And it seemed, the more dangerous the snake, the greater the appeal to Rudy. In his résumé, Rudy describes himself as an expert on the subject of poisonous snakes and other reptiles. He has lectured on the subject at state fairs in Pennsylvania and New York and worked in New York at *The Great Escape* in Lake George; the Bronx Zoo; and the Staten Island Zoo. He once appeared on the national television programs *What's My Line* and The *Johnny Carson Tonight Show*. Rudy has worked with law enforcement agencies on cases involving the illegal importation of reptiles and has extracted venom from some of the most poisonous reptiles for medical research. In 1991, he received a letter of appreciation from The Surgeon General of the U.S. Army for "...assistance to the preventive medicine effort during Operation Desert Shield/Desert Storm. ... and cooperation in helping to provide training materials for field forces."[207]

On the negative side, one of the specie of snakes that Rudy has hunted all his life, the timber rattlesnake (or *Crotalus horridus*), is on the endangered/threatened species listings in all the northeastern states. In 1993,

Rudy was convicted of federal felony charges for trafficking in protected wildlife, *viz.*, the timber rattlesnake. The following year, an article was published in the *Bulletin of the Chicago Herpetological Society* entitled: "A Case in Herpetological Conservation: Notorious Poacher Convicted of Illegal Trafficking in Timber Rattlesnakes."[208] In this article, the authors detailed the negative effects of Rudy's actions, particularly on the survival and status of timber rattlesnake populations of New York and Massachusetts. They also reported of a 1992 grand jury indictment, subsequent arrest, and four month sentence to the federal prison at Allenwood, Pennsylvania. Rudy wrote a rebuttal[209] and his arguments were repudiated by the authors.[210]

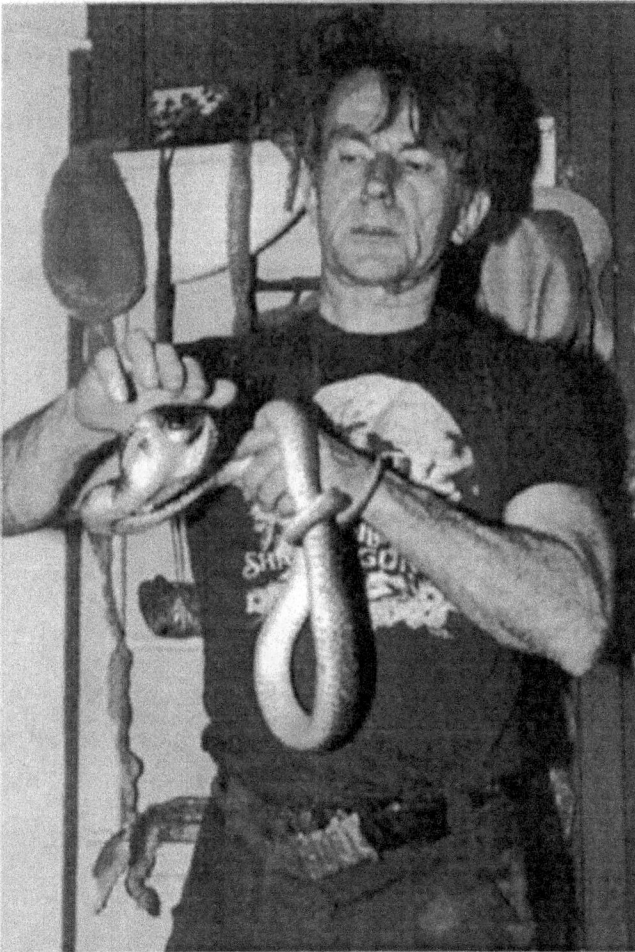

Fig. IV-52. Rudolph Komarek handling a cobra snake, circa 1980's.

Rudy's snake hunting exploits were reported in 1995 on the front page of the *Wall Street Journal*: "For years, this 67 year old outlaw [Rudolph Komarek] has plundered the dens of timber rattlesnakes, earning extra cash by selling the slithery contraband to collectors and pet stores."[211]

In 1995 and 1996, *The News-Chronicle* of Shippensburg, Pennsylvania ran two articles about Rudy: (1) "Rudy the Rattler Wrangler"[212] and "State Sinks Fangs in Snake Man."[213] In the latter, it was reported that on 10 June 1995, the first day of rattlesnake hunting season in Pennsylvania, Rudy took a CNN (Cable News Network) camera crew with him and caught two timber rattlesnakes — one above the state limit. According to the article, in response to the resulting charge, *viz.*, revocation of his snake hunting license, Rudy said, "They're all just jealous because they didn't get to be in the CNN movie."

At present, Rudy travels between the Caribbean, Florida, Pennsylvania and New Jersey, seeking something. In November of 1998 he became a septuagenarian, yet he is in excellent health, takes special care of his diet, lifts weights, and hikes almost daily.

Fig. IV-53. Rudy Komarek, aka "The Cobra King," and snake in 1995.

Robert Edwin Komarek (1932-   )

Robert Edwin Komarek was born on Friday, 07 October 1932 in the Hackensack Hospital. His earliest years were spent at the family home at 62 Marshall Avenue in Little Ferry. After finishing grammar school there, Bob began high school in the nearby town of Lodi. (Little Ferry did not have their own high school.) Before the start of his senior year in 1949, the Komarek family relocated to Ridgewood and Bob became a student at Ridgewood High School.

Following high school graduation, Bob joined the New Jersey National Guard. He served for ten years and retired in 1960 as Staff Sergeant.

Fig. IV-54. Robert Komarek and Sally Ann (née French) Komarek circa mid 1960's.

During his senior year at Ridgewood High, Bob met Sally French. Five years later, on Saturday, 17 September 1955, at Christ Church in Ridgewood, Robert Komarek and Sally Ann French were wed.

In the years to come, Bob and Sally became parents to two children: Bonnie Jean Komarek, born 02 December 1957 in The Valley Hospital, Ridgewood, New Jersey, and Robert John Komarek, born 18 July 1959, also in The Valley Hospital. In their early years, the family resided in the Allwood section of

Clifton, New Jersey. In 1959, the Komereks relocated to Old Bridge, New Jersey, where they purchased a new home.

Fig. IV-55. Bonnie Jean Komarek, Sally Ann (née French) Komarek, Robert Edwin Komarek, and Robert John Komarek circa mid 1960's.

Following in his father's footsteps, Robert became an electrical contractor. He joined the Electricians Union Local No. 3 of New York City, and, after a five year apprenticeship and additional schooling, in 1957 Bob became an Electrician Journeyman. For the next twenty-four years, he was a prime contractor with the firm of Fishback and Moore of New York City. Starting as a Journeyman, Bob quickly progressed to General Superintendent, overseeing such projects as the Repertory Theater at Lincoln Center, the Four Seasons Restaurant/Seagrams Building, New York City Subway Signal System, and a 320 million gallon per day waste water treatment plant. In 1978 and 1979, Robert Komarek negotiated contracts for Fishback and Moore throughout the northeastern United States.

In 1971, Bob, Sally, and their children moved into the Komarek family home at 281 Van Emburgh Avenue in Ridgewood, Bob having purchased the real estate from his father. Eight years later, after many annual trips to the more temperate climate of Florida, the Komareks decided to leave the harsh winters of northern New Jersey and relocate to Redington Shores, Florida. Bob left Fishback and Moore and began his own business, *Tri-lectric*. It became a successful operation with a branch office in Merritt Island, Florida, managed by daughter, Bonnie Jean Komarek.

Some of their projects included industrial and commercial work at Patrick Air Force Base, the Space Flight Center at Cape Kennedy, and numerous senior health care facilities exceeding one million dollars.

Unfortunately, in 1986 and 1987, Robert and Sally experienced irreconcilable, marital difficulties. In 1990 they divorced and *Tri-lectric* closed its doors. Bob then spent a year working as a Contracting Personnel Recruiter, securing positions for large construction companies nationwide. Sally Ann (née French) Komarek continued to reside in North Redington Beach.

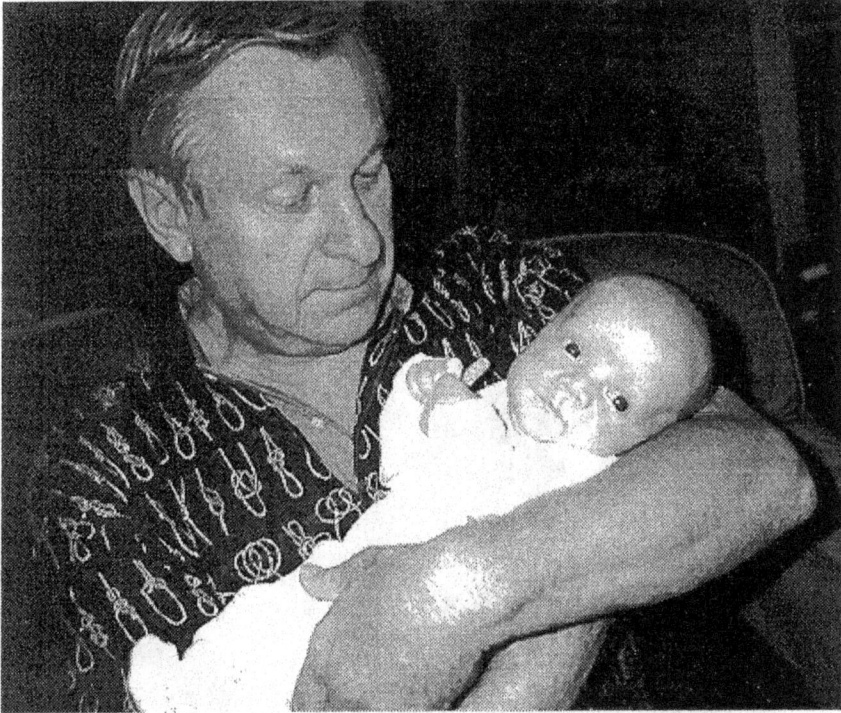

Fig. IV-56. Robert Edwin Komarek and grandson, Ryan Samuel Hall.

In 1990 Bob met Stephanie (née Pieper) Garner. Stephanie was born in West Palm Beach, Florida, but reared in northern New York, only seventy-two miles from Montreal. In 1965, Stephanie returned to Florida. This was brought about by a transfer of her then husband, an agent with the Federal Bureau of Investigation. A mother of four, Stephanie is very successful in the field of interior design. She routinely works in homes valued in the million dollar bracket.

Robert and Stephanie live together as POSSLQs,[214] in Clearwater, on the western coast of central Florida. They share an interest in the field of construction, trade shows, and model centers, touring museums, traveling, and the theater. In 1993, Robert formed a new electrical company, Falcon Electric,

Incorporated of Tampa, Florida. It is a rapidly growing enterprise with a very promising future.

Fig. IV-57. Robert Edwin Komarek and Stephanie (née Pieper) Garner circa early 1990's.

Fig. IV-58. Frances (née Rucker) Skelton, Francesca (née Fried) (Rudich) Skelton, Mary (née Rucker) Frotscher, Robert Komarek, and Stephanie Garner. (Photo taken 14 June 1997.)

Fig. IV-59. Frances (née Rucker) Skelton, Rudy Komarek, Bill Frotscher, Robert Komarek, and Mary (née Rucker) Frotscher. (Photo taken 14 June 1997.)

William Franklin Frotscher, Jr. (1934-   )

William and Mary (née Rucker) Frotscher had only one child: William Franklin Frotscher, Jr. Bill, as he is called, was born on Friday, 12 January 1934 in the Hackensack Hospital.

Until his graduation from high school, the only home Bill knew was the Frotscher residence at 153 Fairmont Avenue in Maywood, another small New Jersey town located about three miles northwest of the Rucker home in Little Ferry.

Bill recounted with some sadness, the changes his boyhood neighborhood has undergone over the years in a historical reflective account published in 1993.[215]

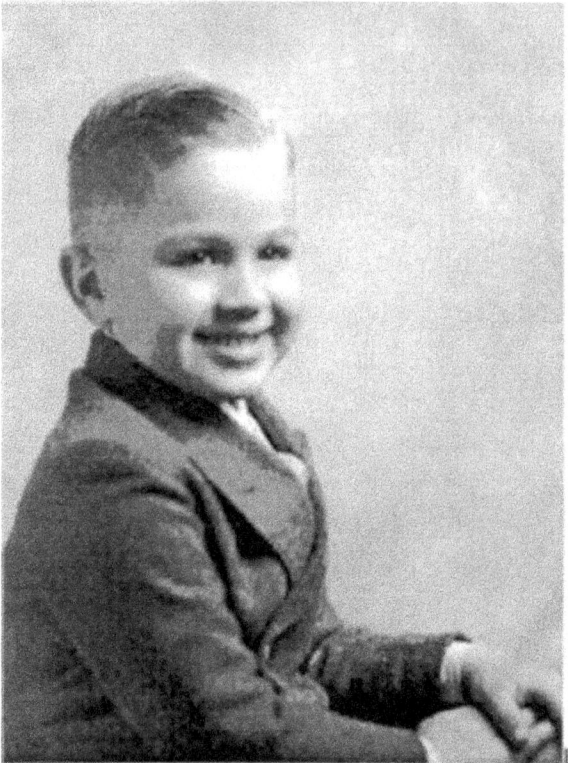

Fig. IV-60. Bill at about 5 years of age.

As with many boys, a primary focal point of Bill's early years was athletics. A natural attraction for sports was enhanced by a gift to excel. His distinction in athletics was exhibited on the football fields and basketball courts, but nowhere else did it shine more brightly than on the baseball diamond. Unfortunately when fourteen, Bill sustained a serious injury to his knee. This effectively ended his participation in competitive sports.

It may have been this excellence in athletics that led to a strong sense of self confidence and a demonstration of his leadership abilities. He was captain of many of the teams on which he played, elected president of his class at school for six consecutive years, and served as captain of the Safety Patrol for almost three years. Upon graduation from junior high school, Bill was the recipient of the highest scholastic award for boys, the National Scholastic Achievement Award sponsored by the American Legion. Later, as a student in Bogota High School, Bill was chosen to represent his class on the Student Council and served in school service organization. He was selected as master-of-ceremonies for his class' graduation day production.

While in his early teen years, Bill became an active member of the Boy Scouts of America. Here too he was outstanding. An article with the following headline appeared in the *Bergen Evening Record* on 07 February 1950: "William Frotscher To Serve As Mayor As Scouts Take Over Town Government." The occasion was Boy Scout Civic Day, part of the fourteenth observance of Scouting in America. The article went on to say, that "...William Frotscher of 153 Fairmont Avenue, a member of Troop No. 77, will serve as the chief executive of the Borough." Sometime after that, Bill received Scouting's highest award: Eagle.

During his years in Bogota High, Bill also had a part-time job in landscape gardening. In some way, this molded the direction his life was to take. Combining this with his other natural interests in hunting and fishing, led Bill into a career in forestry. Following his graduation from high school in 1952, Bill entered Paul Smith's College located in Paul Smiths, New York. He received an Associate's degree in 1954 and, before continuing his education, elected to enter the armed service. At this time, the country was deeply involved in the Korean War. Bill placed himself on active duty status with the U.S. Army Reserve unit he had joined while at Paul Smith's.

Following basic training at Fort Dix, New Jersey, Bill was detailed to Fort Belvoir, Virginia for sixteen weeks of training as an Engineer Heavy Equipment Repairman. Following that, he was assigned to Ladd Air Force Base in Fairbanks, Alaska, where he served out the remainder of his military obligation. His final time in the Army was spent as the clerk of his company.

Given an honorable discharge, Bill resumed academic pursuits in the forestry program at the University of Maine in Orono. Two years later he was awarded a B.S. degree in forestry. He was considering graduate work and had been offered a scholarship from Purdue University. He also had several attractive job offers and decided to begin applying the lessons he had been learning in school to life. In 1958, Bill accepted a position with the Pennsylvania Department of Forests and Waters in McConnelsburg, Pennsylvania.

Not long after moving to McConnelsburg, Bill met Cherry (née Winford) Cooper, then a home economist at the county extension home. The couple married in 1959 in Chester, Pennsylvania and then began building a life together.

Fig. IV-61. Cherry (née Winford) (Cooper) Frotscher and William Franklin Frotscher, Jr. (center), Earl Franklin Skelton (second from far right), Robert Edwin Komarek (far right), *et al.* taken 01 August 1959 in Chester, Pennsylvania.

Their first child, Susan Frances Frotscher, was born in 1963 in Waynesboro, Pennsylvania. Their next child, William Franklin Frotscher-III, was born five years later. Tragically, he contracted leukemia and died at the tender age of two. Unable to have any more natural children, Bill and Cherry elected to adopt. Next to join the Frotscher family was David.

Shortly thereafter, Jennifer became the fourth child to join the Frotscher clan. She was born in 1973 in the Republic of South Korea, but unfortunately with a defective heart. In 1977, Jennifer underwent open heart surgery to correct the birth defect. The operation was successful, but complications developed from the drugs used to keep her body from rejecting the materials used to repair her defective heart. This left her with an inability to ward off infection and she died shortly after the surgery due to a massive lung infection. She was only four.

The last addition to the family was Lynelle, who also was born in the Republic of South Korea. That was on 01 August 1974. Lynelle turned out to be a very high spirited and independently minded young lady.

Following a few years working for the Commonwealth of Pennsylvania, Bill struck out on his own. He started his own business called Penn Forestry Company, Inc. This led to a broad variety of business ventures, most of which centered around providing forest management services to those who owned forest land, but were unable or unwilling to hire their own forester. A one-hundred acre family Christmas tree farm was one positive offshoot of this.

Some time later, Bill owned and operated a logging and pulpwood cutting business. He had tractor trailers which hauled all types of forestry products around the northeastern section of the United States He also had a fleet of excavating equipment which was used for various environmental operations.

Fig. IV-62. Sue and Bill on 27 May 1986.

Unfortunately, after twenty-eight years and many complications, the marriage between Bill and Cherry ended in divorce. Cherry has maintained an active relationship with her former mother-in-law, Mary, and Mary's sister, Frances, providing them with much help and comfort.

On 20 August 1988 in Newburg, Pennsylvania, Bill remarried. His new wife is Sarah Anne (née Hamilton) Buttermore. Known to family and friends as "Sue," she was born on 26 June 1945 at Fort Benning, Georgia. Following graduation in 1963 from Conneaut Valley High School in Conneautville, Pennsylvania, Sue entered Pennsylvania State University. She received a B.A. degree from there in 1967 and went on to earn two advanced degrees, a Masters in Fine Arts in 1970, also from Penn State, and a Masters in Education, from Shippensburg University in 1995. She is currently teaching eighth grade for children with learning disabilities at Faust Junior High School in Chambersburg, Pennsylvania. Following her retirement from teaching, Sue plans to pursue a career as a professional artist.

Today, Sue and Bill continue to live on the family Christmas tree farm, known as Pine Tree Farm, a short distance from the home of Mary (née Rucker) Frotscher. Bill is semi-retired, keeping his hand in one or two forestry related business ventures and maintaining a consulting forestry business operated under the business name: William F. Frotscher, Professional Forester.

Earl Franklin Skelton (1940-   )

    Floyd and Frances (née Rucker) Skelton also had only one child, Earl Franklin Skelton, known to the family as "Skip". He was born on 08 April 1940 in the Hackensack Hospital and grew up in the adjacent town of Teaneck.

Fig. IV-63. Edward Rucker (seated at the left), Earl ("Skippy") Franklin Skelton (front center), William Franklin Frotscher, Sr. (back center), Mary (née Rucker) Frotscher, and Frances (née Rucker) Skelton (far right), taken circa 1947 at the Frotscher home at 153 Fairmont Avenue, Maywood, New Jersey.

    Skip graduated from Teaneck High School in 1958, from Fairleigh Dickinson University in 1962 with a B.S. in Physics, and from Rensselaer Polytechnic Institute in 1967 with a Ph.D. in Physics. He next accepted a Postdoctoral Associateship from the National Research Council and began work as a research physicist at the U. S. Naval Research Laboratory (NRL) in Washington, DC.

    In 1976, Dr. Skelton was promoted to Head of the Phase Transformation Section at NRL and two years later, was invited to serve as a Liaison Scientist in the Office of Naval Research at the U.S. Embassy in Tokyo. In 1980-81, he took a sabbatical at the Stanford Synchrotron Radiation Laboratory at Stanford University in Palo Alto, California.

He has been an invited speaker at scientific conferences around the world and has held academic positions at Prince George's Community College, the University of Maryland, the University of Hawaii at Manoa, and The George Washington University, where today, he is an Adjunct Professor in the Department of Physics and a Professorial Lecturer in the School of Engineering and Applied Science.

Dr. Skelton has authored or co-authored over three-hundred publications. Most are scientific research papers; others include a monograph,[216] an encyclopedia article,[217] a book chapter,[218] and five patents.[219] He has received seven awards for his scientific publications from NRL and in 1979, was given the *Yuri Gagarin Award* and Medal by the U.S.S.R. In 1980, he was elected a *Fellow* of the American Physical Society and in 1995, the Thomas Edison Chapter of *Sigma Xi, The Scientific Research Society*, selected him to receive their *Pure Science Award*. That event was recognized in the *U.S. Congressional Record.*[220] In 1997, he was the recipient of the U.S. Navy's *Technology Transfer Award*.

In 1992, Earl won the National Genealogical Society's "Family History Writing Contest,"[221] and three years later, he published his first family history book.[222] In 1997, he was examined and certified by the Board for Certification of Genealogists.[223]

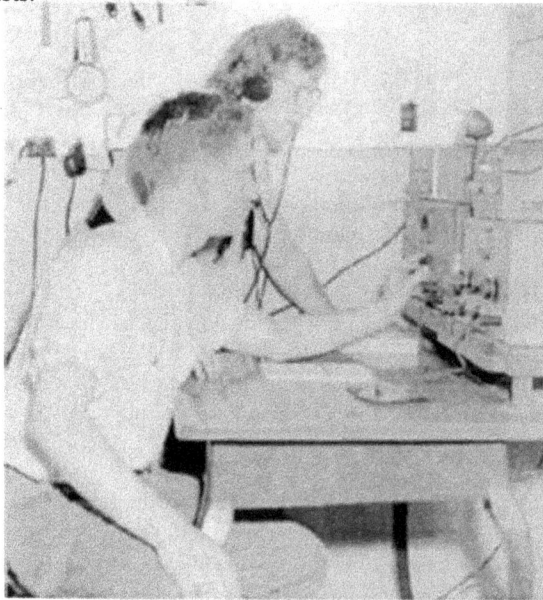

Fig. IV-64. "Earl Skelton of Teaneck
tunes in receiver as mother listens."[224]

Earl has had a long time interest in amateur radio communication. First licensed in 1955 as *KN2OOJ*, today his radio call sign contains his initials, *N3ES*. In 1957, the *Bergen Evening Record* ran an article about him in their weekend magazine.[225] Twenty-four years later, he combined his interests in amateur radio and long distance running. In collaboration with fellow hams from the NRL Amateur Radio Club, Earl tried to gain entry into the *Guinness Book of World Records* by becoming the first person to complete a 26.2 mile marathon foot race — while simultaneously conducting two-way radio communications with other hams around the world. This feat was reported in *The Washington Post*[226] and local newspapers,[227] in *Runner's World* and other running magazines,[228] and in national amateur radio journals.[229] (The editors of *Guinness* rejected the submission, claiming that it was too complicated and that there was no basis of comparison.[230])

Fig. IV-65. Skip and Carol at a cookout in 1958.

In the spring of 1958, Skip met Carol Nettie Reder. The story of how they fell in love and endured a tumultuous courtship, sadly being forced apart by Carol's parents, is detailed in a short story entitled *Carol's Legacy*.[231]

Following their breakup, Carol died from lupus erythematosus — she was only twenty years old. Her remains are interred in the George Washington Park Memorial Cemetery in Paramus, New Jersey.

On 17 June 1962, in Hackensack, Earl married Anita Patton. The marriage lasted twenty years and produced two children: Diana and Isaac.

Fig. IV-66. Taken at the wedding of Earl and Anita on 17 June 1962 in Hackensack. From left to right: Earl Skelton, Mary (née Rucker) Frotscher, Anita (née Patton) Skelton, Vivian Rainman [later Kirshner], William F. Frotscher, Sr., Gertrude (née Feldrais) Patton, and Edward Rucker.

In May 1982, Anita aborted the marriage and the family. Diana remained with her father, while Anita took Isaac to live with her elsewhere in Washington. Sometime later, Anita moved (with Isaac) to Glen Echo, Maryland and then to California, where she began cohabitation with her lover and former boss, a man who had left his wife and infant son. The move to California was very upsetting to Isaac; he chose to return to Washington to live with his father.

Several years later, Earl met and fell in love with Thelma Francesca (née Fried) Rudich. Francesca and Earl were married on 19 October 1986 in Washington. At the time of their marriage, Isaac was fourteen years old; as the wife of the custodial parent, Francesca helped raise Isaac to adulthood.

Francesca grew up in the Bronx Borough of New York City. In 1956, at the age of sixteen, she graduated from Theodore Roosevelt High School. (Her early high school graduation was because she was in an accelerated program for gifted students.) On 15 June 1960, she received a B.S. degree in biology from The College of the City of New York (CCNY). At that time, students admitted to CCNY received full tuition scholarships. Women were barred from college sports teams then, so Francesca went out for the CCNY Cheerleading Squad. She won a coveted berth on the squad and then was elected to head the group for several years. While she was squad captain, the group was highlighted in several newsreels in movie theaters, a popular way to present the news at that time.

Francesca's first husband was David Akivah Rudich and with him she had two children: Bradley Joseph Rudich and Phylisa (Lisa) Kay Rudich.[232] Both children are now grown. Brad is a successful artist and Lisa is a television producer and director. Francesca left David after eighteen years of marriage. She was happy in the single life for ten years, before meeting Earl and being swept off her feet by him in the spring of 1985.

Fig. IV-67. T. Francesca (née Fried) (Rudich) Skelton and Earl Franklin Skelton taken in October 1993 in Agra, India.

While her children were young, Francesca took graduate courses at Hofstra University, was active in several environmental groups, and was elected president of the Bowie [Maryland] Chapter of Zero Population Growth (ZPG). She was an invited speaker before many groups, was the subject of local newspaper articles, and made appearances on radio talk shows.

After her children were in school, Francesca began working as a technical writer for the Naval Ordinance Laboratory in White Oak, Maryland. She broke new ground as the first woman to be hired into a group of male technical writers and received several awards for her work. She then worked as a Public Affairs Specialist at Coast Guard Headquarters in Washington. In addition to her normal duties, she was the Coast Guard representative for special projects for The Honorable Elizabeth Dole, then Secretary of Transportation, for whom she prepared press releases, *inter alia.* Francesca also was active in upgrading the status of women. She received several awards for her work, some from Secretary Dole. Among these awards was one for running workshops to help the advancement of women. During her government career, Francesca also did free-lance writing and continues that today.

On lunch hours during their courtship, Earl would run the twelve mile round trip between NRL to the Coast Guard Headquarters to bestow favors on his heart's delight and to ward off competition at the Coast Guard. Francesca seemed to be impressed with his "running form," as well as the love letters with which he showered her. Today, Francesca and Earl live happily in their home in the Chevy Chase section of Washington, DC.

Ninth Generation

Bonnie Jean (née Komarek) Hall (1957-   )

Bonnie Jean Komarek is the older child of Robert Edwin Komarek and Sally Ann French, his wife. Bonnie was born on 02 December 1957 at The Valley Hospital in Ridgewood, New Jersey. She was raised in northern New Jersey, but later relocated with her family to Florida.

On 04 January 1992, at The Church by the Sea in Madeira Beach, Pinellas County, Florida, Bonnie Jean married John F. Hall. John was born on 27 August 1953 in Maryland and is a national marketing director for a bakery products company in Chicago. Bonnie is a project manager for Kelso Barnett.

On 27 June 1995, Bonnie and John added the next generation to this segment of the family: Ryan Samuel Hall was born in Glendale Heights, Illinois. A second son, Patrick, was born in the fall of 1997.

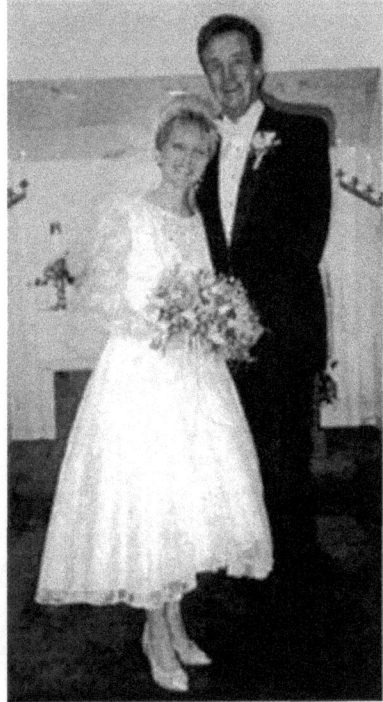

Fig. IV-68. Bonnie Jean (née Komarek) Hall and John Hall on 04 January 1992.

Fig. IV-69. Mrs. Bonnie Hall and her father, Robert Edwin Komarek on 04 January 1992 in Madeira Beach, Florida.

Robert John Komarek (1959-   )

Robert John Komarek was born on 18 July 1959, also at The Valley Hospital in Ridgewood, New Jersey. Robert was reared in northern New Jersey. On 23 December 1985, in Ponce, Puerto Rico, he married Maria Falcon. Today they reside in Lake Okeechobee, Florida where Robert is a contractor as a wet land mitigator.

Fig. IV-70. Robert John Komarek and Marie (née Falcon) Komarek on 23 December 1985 in Ponce, Puerto Rico.

Susan Frances (née Frotscher) (Collson) Heberlig (1963-   )

Susan Frances Frotscher, known to family as "Susy" and to friends as "Sue", was born on 22 May 1963 in Waynesboro, Pennsylvania, to parents Bill and Cherry Frotscher.

She grew up on the family Christmas tree farm in Newburg, Pennsylvania. She was active in school, particularly in music and drama, as well as at church, participating in the youth group and choir at the Newburg United Methodist Church. It was here that her romance with Lance William Heberlig began.

Lance's plans and goals centered mainly around owning and operating the Heberlig family pig farm in Newburg. Susan planned to attend college and to sample city life after eighteen years of rural Pennsylvania, so Lance and Susan parted.

At Lycoming College in Williamsport, Pennsylvania, Susan met and developed a relationship with Jeffrey Goodman Collson, a smart and responsible individual who promised to make a good companion for striking out into the wide world.

Susan and Jeff married in 1985 and moved to Alexandria, Virginia, just outside of Washington, DC. Susan worked as a paralegal for a Georgetown law firm, while Jeff worked as a tennis instructor, a retail manager for a sporting goods store, and obtained a teaching certificate from George Mason University in Fairfax, Virginia.

Tiring quickly of city life, and wishing to purchase a home, in 1990 they moved to Kernersville, North Carolina, a suburb of Winston-Salem. Susan continued as a paralegal, while Jeff taught elementary school physical education.

In 1992, Susan and Jeff separated due to irreconcilable differences. This led to a divorce and the following year, the romance between Susan and Lance was rekindled.

Susan Frotscher and Lance William Heberlig were married on 30 April 1994 at the Newburg United Methodist Church, where their mutual attraction had begun, many years earlier. Today they reside happily on the Heberlig family's pig farm. Susan continues as a paralegal for a Harrisburg law firm, while Lance operates the family farm and also is employed by a popular farm and suburban store named Agway, Incorporated.

On Monday, 16 June 1997, Sue and Lance became parents. William Franklin Heberlig was born in Carlisle Hospital, Carlisle, Pennsylvania.

Fig. IV-71. Susan Frances (née Frotscher) (Collson) Heberlig and Lance
William Heberlig taken 30 April 1994 in Chambersburg, PA.

Fig. IV-72.   Susan Frances (née Frotscher) (Collson) Heberlig, Lance William
Heberlig, and William Franklin Heberlig in August 1997.

Diana (née Diane) Lynne (née Skelton) Faujour (1965-   )

Born in the Samaritan Hospital in Troy, New York on 23 September 1965, Diana Lynne was the first child of Earl and Anita (née Patton) Skelton. Due to her mother's tutelage, when Diana entered kindergarten in 1970, she was tested as reading at the fifth grade level. She skipped a year in the public schools and, in 1976, began studying French. In 1980, she spent her fifteenth summer working as an *au pair* girl for a family in Brittany, on the western coast of France. Her tasks involved housework and child care.

Following graduation from the Washington International School, Diana, a National Merit Scholar Semi-Finalist, was accepted into Cornell University. While there, she earned academic plaudits on the Dean's List and worked her way up from reporter to Managing Editor of *The Cornell Daily Sun*, a self-supporting paper, run by the students of Cornell. She graduated in 1986 with a B.A. in history and Soviet Studies. She also studied three more languages: Hungarian, Russian, and Spanish.

In her earlier years, Diana worked in a children's soup kitchen in one of the poorer sections of Washington, and in the *Reading Is Fundamental* program, which promotes reading in poor neighborhoods. She decided to make a full-time, life commitment to helping the less fortunate. In 1986, she joined the Fourth World Movement Volunteer Corps. The "FW Movement" is dedicated to the war against extreme poverty in the United States and around the world.

During the past decade, Diana has worked both in France and the U.S. She began by working with an itinerant mechanics and computer workshop for teenagers whose families lived in trailers, without water or electricity, scavenging for scrap metal to earn their living. Through the workshop, the young people learned to build generators, and thereby provided their families with electricity. They then sought out even more disadvantaged teenagers to share what they had learned.

In 1988-89, Diana co-researched a report commissioned by the European Economic Community on conditions of poverty in six European countries in view of defining an international anti-poverty policy. (Although the French and Belgian governments have officially adopted the anti-poverty measures drafted by the FW Movement, Europe has done so only partially.)

Diana also translated two books written in French by the FW Movement's founder: *Blessed Are You the Poor* (published in English in 1992) and a second book whose English publication is pending.

During 1991-1995, Diana edited the monthly *Fourth World Youth Journal* in French and English. In this, very poor young people, some of whom cannot read or write, are given the opportunity — many of them for the first time in their lives — to express their opinions and to share with young people of other backgrounds what their experiences in extreme poverty have taught them.

She also represented the FW Movement in the European Union's Youth Forum, serving on the steering committee of its Pilot Project Against Social Exclusion, which allocated financial and moral support to innovative anti-poverty projects in fifteen European countries.

In 1989, Diana married Patrice Yves Faujour, a French metal-worker and tradesman, trained in carpentry, masonry, plumbing and electrical wiring. Patrice was born on 06 December 1957 in Nantes, Loire-Atlantique, France, the son of Claude Yves Faujour and his wife, Therese Henriette Augereau. It is fitting that he married into the family of Rudy Komarek, the snake hunter, because Patrice's first employment, from age 8 to 15, was catching live vipers, which he then sold for five francs each to the Pasteur Institute for their venom antidotes.

When he was nineteen, Patrice, a pedestrian, was flung by a hit-and-run driver 53 yards through the air, according to the police report. He went into a coma that lasted forty days, during which he underwent micro-brain surgery. In the hospital for over eight and one-half months, Patrice had to re-learn to walk, talk, read and write (just as did Harrison Ford in *Regarding Henry*).

When Patrice was twenty-one, he managed to track down the address of his mother, from whom he had been separated at the age of eight, after his parents' divorce. (The judge's custody decision forbade the mother to have any contact with her children.) Despite such a long separation, Patrice was able to rebuild a close and loving relationship with his mother, as well as with her second husband and their three children.

Patrice's second escape from death came at age 29. He was working with a road crew laying a pipe-line. His boss decided to save time by not putting barriers against the walls of the twelve-foot-deep ditch. Patrice was alone at the bottom when the dirt walls began caving in. He was buried up to his chest by the time a crane swiveled over for him to catch onto. The crane pulled him out wearing only his shirt and jockey shorts, as his pants and boots were caught in the cave in!

In 1988, at the age of 30, Patrice chose to work with the FW Movement, organizing work-and-training camps where young people of both underprivileged and highly privileged backgrounds live and do manual work together, learning from one another's life experiences. This is how he and Diana met. They were married in 1989 — twice. Their first wedding, a civil ceremony, attended largely by their French family and friends, was held on 24 June in Cox, Midi-Pyrenees, France. Two months later, on 20 August, they were married again, this time before a rabbi in Washington, DC.

They have been blessed with two beautiful daughters: Joline Mariya, born 31 January 1991 in Silver Spring, Maryland, and Delora Kathline, born 07 December 1993 in Melun, Seine-et-Marne, France. During the period 1991-96, the Faujours lived in Champeaux, France; in the summer of 1996 they relocated to Brooklyn, New York City. Currently, Diana is serving as the Fourth World Permanent Representative to the United Nations and Patrice works at the Fourth World House in lower Manhattan. On two occasions, Diana has spoken formally on behalf of the U.N. World Health Organization's International Congress: first in Ireland in 1996 and most recently in Baltimore, Maryland in 1997."[233],[234] In May 1998, Patrice was awarded a High School Equivalency Diploma from The University of the State of New York.[235]

Fig. IV-73. Diana L. (née Skelton) Faujour and Patrice Faujour
taken 20 August 1989 in Washington, DC.

Fig. IV-74. Family photo taken on 20 August 1989 in Washington, DC.

Fig. IV-74a. Identifier for the grouphotograph (Fig. IV-73).

1. Cherry (née Winford) (Cooper) Frotscher
2. David Daniel Frotscher
3. Lynelle Jean Frotscher
4. Mary (née Rucker) Frotscher
5. Sue (née Hamilton) (Buttermore) Frotscher
6. Jeffrey Goodman Collson
7. William Franklin Frotscher, Jr.
8. Susan Frances (née Frotscher) (Collson) Heberlig
9. Isaac Patton Skelton
10. Frances (née Rucker) Skelton
11. Steven Holmgren
12. Anita (née Patton) (Skelton) Holmgren
13. Diana Lynne (née Skelton) Faujour

14. Earl Franklin Skelton
15. Patrice Yves Faujour
16. Thelma Francesca (née Fried) (Rudich) Skelton
17. Aaron Rosenstreich
18. Bradley Joseph Rudich
19. Benjamin Holmgren
20. Gertrude (née Feldrais) Patton
21. Sheldon Roseman
22. Raissa Patton
23. Judy (née Patton) Rosenstreich
24. Deirdre Patton

David Daniel Frotscher (1971-   )

David was born on 18 October 1971 in Williamsport, Pennsylvania. He was adopted by his parents William Franklin Frotscher and Cherry (née Winford) (Cooper) Frotscher in 1972. He seems to have been gifted with a mechanical aptitude from his natural father. He also learned much about mechanical systems at the knees of his adopted father and grandfather, while growing up on the family Christmas tree farm in Newburg, Pennsylvania.

During David's school years, he was very active in sports. He played midget football and worked his way up through three levels of Little League Baseball. When no longer eligible to play in the youth leagues, he played slow-pitch softball for a local team until he sustained a knee injury requiring hospitalization and surgery.

Fig. IV-75. David Daniel Frotscher and Cherry (née Winford) (Cooper) Frotscher taken in 1994 in Newburg, Pennsylvania.

Dave was also very much involved in musical activities, playing trumpet and drums in both his junior and senior high school bands. His musical accomplishments also included playing the piano and organ for church functions.

Scouting played an important part in Dave's youth. In the fall of 1990, he was awarded Scoutings' highest rank: Eagle. In June 1991, David graduated from Shippensburg High School. [There is a high degree of similarity between the early lives of David and his adopted father: a love and affinity for athletics, curtailment of those activities because of a knee injury, playing the trumpet in the school band, and attainment of the Eagle rank in Boy Scouts.]

Today, David's main recreational interests are hunting and automotive oriented activities. He enjoys attending NASCAR races and has undertaken the building and modification of many high performance pick-up trucks.

Currently he is employed by the Grove Manufacturing Company, a firm involved in the fabrication of hydraulic cranes used worldwide. His duties include the final testing of the cranes and calibration of the computer operated systems prior to shipment.

Isaac Patton Skelton (1971-   )

[The following text was written by Isaac.]

I was born on Armistice Day, November 11, 1971 at the Columbia Hospital for Women in Washington, DC. I am the second child of Anita Patton and Earl Franklin Skelton. My name, which means "He/God laughs" in Hebrew, was taken from my paternal great- and great-great grandfathers, Isaac Franklin Skelton and Isaac Skelton, respectively. My middle name comes from my maternal grandparents, Gertrude ("Girttel") Feldrais and Kenneth Grayson Patton.

When I was born, our family lived in a house on a cul-de-sac set in Oxon Hill, Maryland, a working class neighborhood close to the southeast border of the District of Columbia. Our house was surrounded by tall, weedy grass and a narrow stretch of woods on one side. There was a real cauldron in those woods where my sister, Diana, and I sometimes played witch and warlock games. Diana and I also spent many an afternoon playing with our family pet, a St. Bernard named Nana. I remember the thick humidity of DC's summers and its mild winters.

I also remember nests of tent caterpillars in the nearby trees and occasionally spotting small garden snakes in the grass. I do not remember the story later told to me of a ground hive of wasps I stumbled into as a toddler. My dad heroically rescued me from attacking swarms of angry wasps, suffering as many stings as I did. The final picture is of father and son, covered head to toe in aching, red welts, sitting naked in a warm bath of calamine lotion prepared by mom.

My hometown of Washington is over 80% people of color; southeast DC is almost one hundred percent. When my mom took me to the grocery store, I remember us being the only white people there. Although my sister went to public school where students were bussed in and out as politicians discussed segregation, I attended private schools: a Montessori kindergarten, Washington International School (briefly), and the city's first racially integrated school (Georgetown Day School). My understanding of the race situation in America was confused and, in retrospect, that was much better than reality. As a young student at Washington International School, I was shown a history book with sketches of all the presidents of the United States. One of those presidents shared the first name of my best friend at the time, Dwight, who was black. Dwight D. Eisenhower looked black to me too... which made sense. So, naturally, I thought the US had already had a black president "a long time ago" and probably lots of others.

My father's father, Floyd, grew up in Kentucky. Floyd was a tinkerer and so are his son and grandson. Even though Floyd suffered from chronic pain through most of his life, he was a skilled carpenter who made beautiful coffee tables, chess boards, and many other pieces of inlaid woodwork. I suspect my father's pre-physics dabblings in ham radio and electronics is a product of this workshop tradition.

My mother, Anita, was born the middle child to a poor Jewish family in Washington Heights, New York. In a step up, the family soon moved across the Hudson River to Teaneck, New Jersey. Anita's mother, Gertrude, though she was Jewish, spent a good deal of her childhood in an orphanage, cut off from her family and her Jewish roots. Gertrude would later keep her children, Bob, Anita, and Judy, home from school on Jewish holidays without knowing what to do to celebrate the holiday. When it came time for Anita to teach her own daughter, she found Judaism compatible with atheism. During the winter holidays, we spun the dradle, hung ornaments on the tree, and exchanged presents, attending services at neither church nor synagogue. We just stayed at home as a family — as Gertrude did with her children — and kept warm by the fire.

My father held vastly more stock in scientific theories, which gladly submit themselves to empirical testing under controlled laboratory conditions, rather than vague religious "mumbo-jumbo," based on corrupted, fragmented texts, which must be accepted either literally or figuratively — it didn't matter — on the basis of faith. Faith was defined as a complete suspension of one's logical understanding of reality. Attitudes not surprising, I suppose, for a Ph.D. physicist and mom.

Faith in science was acceptable because science successfully explained the universe in logical terms. Or, rather, what most people considered to be the universe: all the things you can touch and see or measure, using some instrument to enhance the senses. As a young boy, I wondered why religious people would waste their time trying to prove the existence of God to themselves, let alone to me. You could not even look around the room, I thought, without seeing one of the many tangible creations of science which have improved our life so much... like the television set! As a scientist, my dad held Western religion in contempt for its persecution of those who would measure and perceive a reality, contradictory to the Biblical teachings, but ultimately more meaningful to humanity, such as Galileo, Copernicus, and Darwin.

My own faith in Western science has eroded over the years. Perhaps this was due to an increasing awareness of things like the destructive potential of nuclear missiles and power plants; the ill effects of burning fossil fuels on a large scale and discarding toxic wastes on the environment and the organisms living in it; or even recent theories that artificial immunity induced by scientifically engineered human vaccines and antibodies ultimately produces even more threatening mutant versions of those viruses we sought to eliminate. I also remember reading about the effects of chemical warfare on humans in Remarque's *All Quiet on the Western Front*. The whole world seemed (and seems) to be shackled by the threat of "mutually assured destruction" (MAD: a self-descriptive acronym coined by world leaders during the Cold War), made possible by horrifying bombs invented by scientists.

Or perhaps it was because a purely scientific belief system deals only with understanding nature's hidden truths and putting them to work for a privileged minority of the human race, rather than the quiet, humble introspection of religion. All children eventually begin to ask themselves deeper questions, such as the meaning of life, the source of consciousness, whether we are alone in the universe, and the ethical implications of it all. Astronomers, such as the late Carl Sagan, it seems, come closest out of all the sciences to addressing some of these questions.

On second thought, my father did have something like a spiritual tradition, though that aspect of it was not made explicit. By the time I was born, my father had already uncovered many of its secrets and even attained a certain level of mastery. Earl found in me a willing initiate and began my training at seven years of age. Our prophet was Jim Fixx and the religion was running. Its goal went beyond mere health. At one time, it was to improve one's BPR (best personal record): a no-pressure competition with yourself to strive to do better. Later on, when the burden of always beating one's BPR began to take the fun out of it, the goal became increasing the "L" in "LSD" (Long Slow Distance), the culmination of which is the marathon-26.2 miles - or a marathon in cold rain. But I suspect it was really something else.

My father is an accomplished ascetic. When in the early 1980's my dad lost a great deal of weight and the skin clung loosely to his ribs, I think he discovered the true essence of distance running. He tried explaining it to me, "About five miles into a marathon, I just sit back and focus on a single point way out in front of me. I enter a kind of trance and... when I come out of it, I'm in range of the finish line." It sounds a lot like meditation. Runners often compare themselves to the Benedictine monks who inflicted pain on themselves to reach a holy state — real masochists.

Running demands discipline, endurance, a high tolerance for fatigue, and the gumption to rise at 5 A.M. and drag yourself (and your next of kin) out into freezing temperatures to run in a big circle with a lot of other people crazy enough to do the same thing. But even if one neglected to run for months, the main credo was a body is a temple and one was expected to keep the body free of pollutants. I continue to run to this day. It should be noted that, even as an athlete, my father could not help but to see with a physicists eye: He told me always to run the tangents of the curves in the road in order to reduce the distance of the course.

Figs. IV-76 & -77. Isaac Patton Skelton and his dad following the Cherry Blossom 10-Mile Run in Washington, DC in 1979 (left) and in 1992 (right).

Raised without a traditional religious dogma, my sister and I were free to find our own paths. I followed my sister to Ithaca, I thought, to become a physicist or astronomer. But after two years, I had learned all I hoped to learn about the nature of the known universe in Western scientific terms, and left Cornell with a B.A. in Russian and Soviet Studies - also one of Diana's majors.

My own break with science began, curiously, with vegetarianism. My best friends in high school were vegetarians. Their simple logic was hard to deny, since we humans are animals, and all animals are so much alike, to kill and eat one is akin to cannibalism. Surely other animals do not wish to be enslaved, slaughtered and eaten, though their cries and protests may only come close to those of a human baby.

Eating meat is a violent act. It is also hopelessly unclean. These are true statements no matter how many government inspectors and white lab coats you insert into the equation. Meat is super-high in fat, protein, antibiotics, growth hormones, and bad karma. And abstaining from meat fit in perfectly with the "my body is a temple" credo. I remember seeing shocking photographs of bloody murdered cows and rabbits at an animal rights music festival by the Washington Monument in July, 1988. This line of thinking took me in many new directions and quickly replaced science as my prism, through which I saw the underlying reality of the world. Abstention from eating meat was for me a form of protest through non-action.

I discovered that the principles of non-violence and love for all life - trees and all - were universally accepted by Pythagoreans, Buddhists, Jains,

Taoists, Hindus, Seventh Day Adventists, Essenes-the first Christians, and Russian Dukhobori Christians ("spirit wrestlers"), Orthodox Jews, Gandhians, Tolstoyans, pacifists, animal rights activists and many other groups, but not by scientists. Even the ancient Hebrews may have taken the Old Testament words literally:

Fig. IV-78. Proud father and Isaac Patton Skelton,
on the occasion of Isaac's graduation from
Cornell University on 30 May 1993.

And God said, Behold, I have given you every herb bearing seed, which is upon the face of all the earth, and every tree, in the which is the fruit of a tree yielding seed; to you it shall be for meat. (Genesis 1:29)

On the contrary, scientists view an emotional consideration for life to be wholly unscientific. Such regard for the test subject of a primate psychology experiment, for example, can corrupt otherwise objective data taking. Many scientists in the West defend the wicked practice of revealing truth through torture, calling it "vivisection." My own search for truth led me on a wonderful and so far unfinished journey through Eastern religions and philosophies.

Cornell, famous for an armed student takeover of an administrative building in 1969, was still full of conscience-raising trouble makers twenty years later... and was ripe for more drama. Just three years prior to my arrival at Cornell, a controversial cocaine-addiction experiment involving cats, electrodes, and exposed brain tissue ceased to be funded, after a strong public outrage and protests hit the press. I found the Cornell Students for the Ethical Treatment of Animals (CSETA) chugging along, ran for its presidency and was elected. Our membership grew and the group's energy level shot up.

We invited noted speakers from Feminists for Animal Rights and the Physicians Committee for Responsible Medicine, consulted with Cornell's dining staff on improving the vegetarian choices and hosting an all-veggie night, staged numerous protests and operations against the donkey basketball business, the *foie de gras* business in upstate New York, Cornell's chicken research labs, and General Motors' use of live pigs in crash tests. We also strengthened ties with the superbly-run Farm Sanctuary in nearby Watkins Glen, the largest facility in the world for rescued and rehabilitated farm animals.

My dorm room became a sanctuary for one abused orphan rabbit, whom I called "Peter." Over the course of five years, Peter taught me how to sit quietly, be patient, gentle, caring, and how to improve my diet. Our favorite pastime was rubbing noses together. Rabbits are very wise and skillful herbivores. They are extremely communicative and expressive. Peter died in 1996 of calcium stones and is buried at Farm Sanctuary.

We also started a small publication called *AnimaLife* in 1991, which gave students concerned about animal rights issues a forum for their ideas. By the time I left Cornell, the journal had grown to a full 16-page magazine with a distribution into the thousands. We published an article on "Mad Cow Disease," complete with scientific notations, five years before that story became international news. Today, *AnimaLife* can be read on the World Wide Web by loading the URL address <http://www.envirolink.org/arrs/AnimaLife/> and will score 137 "hits" (references) on an Infoseek <http://www.infoseek.com/> search.

Before leaving Cornell, I participated in a national "March for the Animals" in DC and a conference on the future of animal rights at Rutgers Law School in New Jersey. While in a Master's program at Georgetown University, I presented my thesis on the "Russian Vegetarian Tradition" to a panel at the annual meeting of the American Association for the Advancement of Slavic Studies (AAASS) at Harvard University and again at a University of Connecticut conference.

I am grateful that my nascent professional life has been a fusion of personal interests. Right now I am working in New York as the sole administrator for the US branch of a 14,000+ member peace organization called Servas, a non-profit group established in 1948 to promote peace

through international cultural exchange. My first job was as an intern for
the International Science Foundation (ISF) at their headquarters office in
DC. ISF was a $130 million grants program for scientists of the former
Soviet Union (fSU) funded by the Hungarian-born philanthropist and
financier George Soros. With backgrounds in the physical sciences and
Russian studies, ISF was a great opportunity to help organize scientific
review panels and award research grants to struggling fSU scientists.

Fig. IV-79. Isaac Patton Skelton and Dana (née Sevastyanova) Segal Skelton
immediately after their wedding on 21 October 1996 at the Chapel (Room 257), City
Hall, Manhattan, New York City, New York.

After being promoted to Program Officer and transferred in 1996 to
Soros' Open Society Institute (OSI) in New York, I helped to author the
concluding annual report for that foundation. As a program manger for OSI,

I helped open an Internet center at the Dalnevostochny (Far East) State University in Vladivostok, Russia.

The day before embarking for Vladivostok, I married Dana (pronounced "Donna") Sevastyanova Segal. Dana was born on 18 May 1973 to Lea Segal and Vladimir Sevastyanov in Donetsk, Soviet Socialist Republic of Ukraine.[236] When still only a very young girl, her parents divorced. Dana was raised in Riga, Latvia, by her mother, a chemist, and step-father Leonid (Lenny) Gershanovich, a metallurgist. When she was sixteen, Dana emigrated with her family to the United States where, almost eight years later, they all became naturalized citizens.[237]   Today, Lea and Lenny live in Westchester County, New York.

In May 1997, Dana graduated from Barnard College, Columbia University where she majored in mathematics and statistics. Currently, she is employed as a senior statistical analyst for Moody's Investors Service. On 22 September 1997 in New York, Dana and I became parents to a daughter, Dora Segal Skelton.

It is said that America is the land of mongrels — a menagerie of different tribes from all over the world who left their homelands in search of safety and opportunity. And mutts, though not always pretty, are hardy and resilient... survivors.

Thanks to 19th and 20th century advances in technology, transportation and military hardware, a great migration has ensued. Airplanes and trains bring people together who were previously separated by thousands of years of history and as many miles. Just in the last seventy-five years, many millions of people from across Europe, Asia, the Pacific Islands, Africa and the Americas, who were not killed in wars, have been forced to flee their home towns by generals in the war room and politicians at the negotiating table. Many more have fled oppressive regimes or the specter of starvation. The world has changed so much in so short a time that we can have no idea what the ultimate results will be.

Just fifty years ago, racism and xenophobia, while not ubiquitous, were prevalent enough to scare many struggling immigrants into patterns of assimilation. Parents denied their native language and saw to it that their children spoke English only. Today, immigrant families arrive in the U.S. knowing that the preservation of their native culture and their quest for United States citizenship are not mutually exclusive. America is full of private communities, quarters and neighborhoods of first- and second-generation immigrants all sharing the same language or religion. In some Spanish-speaking communities, the pendulum has even swung in the other direction, where kids are so surrounded by Spanish speakers that, for many, assimilation no longer becomes an option.

My blood is that of previously nomadic Jewish sheep herders who settled down as craftsmen and traders in the provinces of Russia, Kiev and Poland; my bones are passed down from Czech subjects of the Bohemian empire; my organs and hair were given to me by working-class Englishmen who sold themselves into slavery to pay for their voyage to the New World, where they hoped to find freedom and land.

My wife is also descended mainly from the Ashkenazi Jews of Ukraine and Latvia, and from the Eurasian "Russians," strange mixture of Varangian (Norse Viking), Mongol, and Slavic peasantry. Who can say with confidence what sway these diverse genetic forces will have on our daughter, Dora? Each of these peoples I describe above has their own mentality, their own world view, their own humor, their own sense of history, their own adaptations to their environment, their own "nature." Do they combine to form a completely new character, or do they vie for dominance, taking their turn in each stage of growth or in each new generation?

Fig. IV-80. Isaac Patton Skelton, Adolph, aka "Bep," Rucker, Frances (née Rucker) Skelton, and Edward Rucker taken in November 1995 at the Rucker family home in Little Ferry, New Jersey.

Lynelle Jean Frotscher (1974-   )

Lynelle was born on 01 August 1974 in the Republic of South Korea and not long after, was adopted by her American parents, William Franklin Frotscher, Jr. and Cherry (née Winford) (Cooper) Frotscher. A very strong willed and independent young woman, Lynelle left home following her graduation from Shippensburg High School in January 1983 and supported herself as a waitress.

Fig. IV-81. Lynelle Jean Frotscher circa 1991.

On 08 February 1993 in the Chambersburg Hospital in Chambersburg, Pennsylvania, Lynelle gave birth to a son, Matthew Kilgore; two years later, on 22 February 1995, she bore a daughter, Jessica Marie.

Lynelle continues to work full-time as a waitress and lives with her husband, Todd Matthew Kilgore, and their children in a home they have purchased near, Newburg, Pennsylvania. On 02 August 1995, the *News Chronicle* published a photograph featuring five generations of the Todd family.

Fig. IV-82. "Five generations: A recent family gathering of the Kilgore family resulted in the opportunity for a generation photo. Seated, left to right, are Todd Kilgore holding Jessica and Matthew; standing, Joe Kilgore, Trean Kilgore and Minnie Stein.[238]

On 10 January 1997, Lynelle and Todd added a third child to their family, a daughter.

Tenth Generation

Fig. IV-83. Joline Mariya Faujour (b. 31 January 1991) and Delora Kathline Faujour (b. 07 December 1993). The photograph was taken in May 1996 in Baillet-en-France, France.

Despite a hearing loss requiring several ear operations and hearing aids, Joline is now fluent in French and English. She also has begun studying Hebrew and sign language and is in her second year of ballet classes.

Delora loves babies and cats.

Fig. IV-84. Ryan Samuel Hall (b. 27 June 1995)

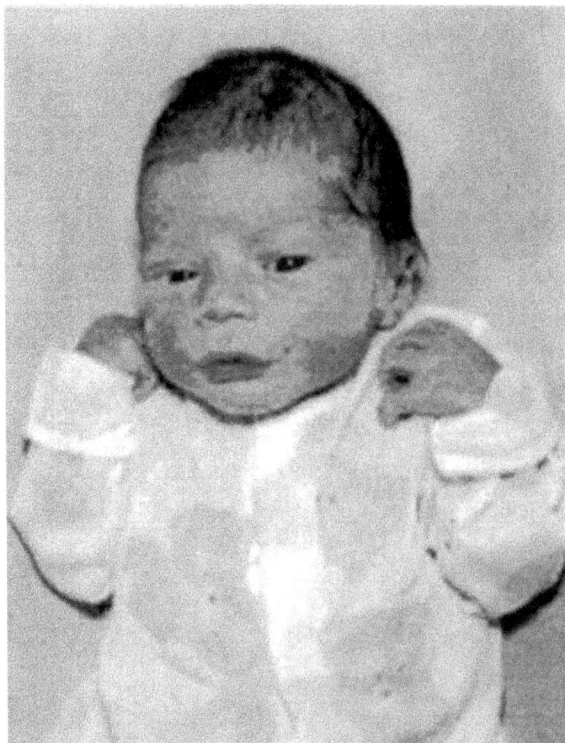

Fig. IV-85.   William Franklin Heberlig (b. 16 June 1997)

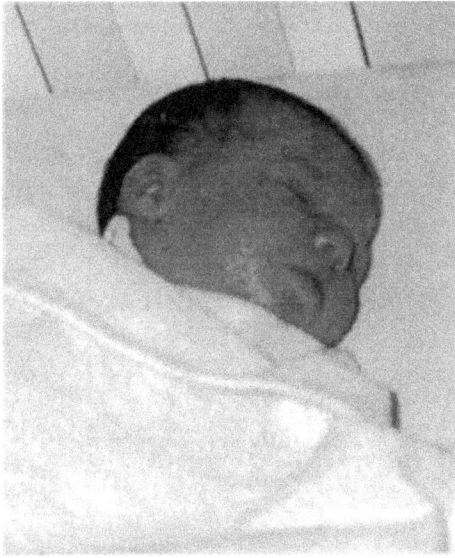

Fig. IV-86. Dora Segal Skelton (b. 22 September 1997)

Fig. IV-87. Mary (née Rucker) Frotscher, Dana (née Sevastyanova) Segal Skelton, Dora Segal Skelton, and Frances (née Rucker) Skelton taken at the home of Mary Frotscher on 28 November 1998.

Family Reunion Photograph - 1996

Fig. IV-88. Family reunion in Chambersburg, Pennsylvania on 23 December 1996.

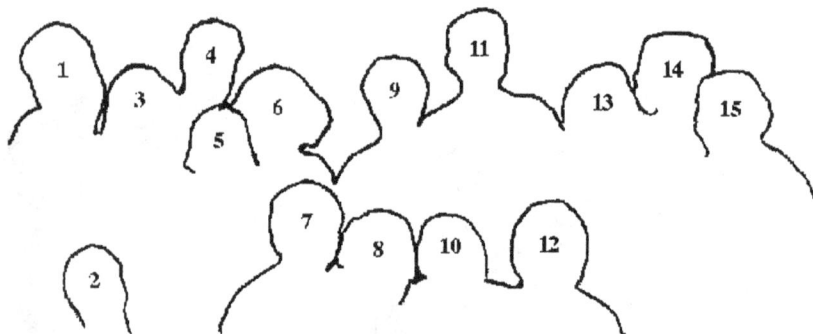

Fig. IV-88a. Identifier for the group photograph (Fig. IV-86).

1. Patrice Yves Faujour
2. Joline Mariya Faujour
3. Diana Lynn (née Skelton) Faujour
4. Isaac Patton Skelton
5. Delora Kathline Faujour
6. Dana (née Sevastyanova) Segal Skelton
7. Earl Franklin Skelton
8. Frances (née Rucker) Skelton
9. Sarah Ann (née Hamilton) (Buttermore) Frotscher

10. Thelma Francesca (née Fried) (Rudich) Skelton
11. William Franklin Frotscher, Jr.
12. Mary (née Rucker) Frotscher
13. Susan Frances (née Frotscher) (Collson) Heberlig
14. Lance William Heberlig
15. Cherry (née Winford) (Cooper) Frotscher

Genealogical Summary: Descendants of Jan Příhoda and Žofie Zimová

1. Jan[1] Příhoda married **Žofie Zimová** on 21 January 1692 in Soběslav in Jižní Čechy Province in southern Bohemia.[239,240] Jan and Žofie were parents to at least six children, all born in Soběslav:[241]

2   i.   Dorotea[2] Příhodova, born 12 December 1701.

3   ii.   František Příhoda, born 20 November 1703.

4   iii.   Thomáš Příhoda, born 12 December 1705.

5   iv.   Jan Příhoda, born 08 May 1708.

6   v.   Josef Příhoda, born 02 February 1711

+   7   vi.   Andreas {Ondřej} Příhoda, baptized 16 November 1713 in Soběslav; married 10 November 1735 in Soběslav, Anna Duchwaldová.

7. Andreas[2] {Ondřej} Příhoda (Jan[1]) born 16 November 1713 in Soběslav;[242] married 10 November 1739 in Soběslav, **Anna Duchwaldová**, daughter of František Duchwald.[243] Only two children of Andreas and Anna are known; there may have been others:[244]

+   8   i.   Martin[3] {Martinus} Příhoda, born 04 October 1753 in Soběslav; died 22 July 1842 in Nedvědice, Jižní Čechy Province; married 04 October 1753 in Soběslav, Marie Cilková.

9   ii.   Mathias Příhoda, born 25 February 1756 in Soběslav.

8. Martin[3] {Martinus} Příhoda (Andreas[2], Jan[1]) born 04 October 1753 in Soběslav;[245] died 22 July 1842 in Nedvědice, Jižní Čechy Province in southern Bohemia, and there buried on 24 July 1842;[246] married 07 February 1780 in Nedvědice No. 24, **Marie** (or **Marie-Anna**) **Cilková**,[247] born 23 December 1758 in Klenovice, Jižní Čechy Province in southern Bohemia, the daughter of Ignatius Cilek and Marianna Neškodná;[248] died 02 November 1796 at Nedvědice No. 24.[249] Martin and Marie (also called "Magdalena") were parents to six children; all were born "from the village Nedvědice No. 24":[250]

+   10   i   Jan[4] Příhoda, born 31 May 1786; married 08 February 1820
              in Soběslav, Sofie {Žofie} Freslová.

     11   ii.   Barbora Příhodova, born 03 December 1788.

     12   iii.   Anežka Příhoda, born 11 January 1790.

     13   iv.   Petr Příhoda, born 27 June 1791.

     14   v.   Antonin Příhoda, born 12 December 1793.

     15   vi.   Eleonora Příhodova, born 15 January 1795.

    10. Jan[4] Příhoda (Martin[3], Andreas[2], Jan[1]) born 31 May 1786 in
Nedvědice No. 24;[251] married 08 February 1820 in Soběslav, **Sofie {Žofie}
Freslová**,[252] born circa 1800 or 1801 in Soběslav No. 34, the daughter of
Karel Fressl and Voršila Ferrová;[253] died 02 August 1848 at Nedvědice No. 24
and buried on 04 August 1848, also in Nedvědice.[254] Jan and Sofie were parents
to seven children, all born in the village of Nedvědice No. 24:[255]

     16   i.   Filipina[5] Příhodova, born 07 August 1821.

     17   ii.   Karel Příhoda, born 15 July 1822. [Since the seventh child
                  of Jan and Sofie, born in 1831, also was named Karel, it is
                  inferred that this child died before that time.]

     18   iii.   Josephus Příhoda, born 09 March 1824.

     19   iv.   Anastasie Příhoda, born 19 April 1825.

     20   v.   Marie Příhodova, born 10 June 1826.

     21   vi.   Francisca Příhodova, born 14 September 1828.

+   22   vii.   Karel Příhoda, born 15 September 1831. Karel had at least
                   two wives: Františka Moravecova and Jana Moravecova.

    22. Karel[5] Příhoda (Jan[4], Martin[3], Andreas[2], Jan[1]) born 15 September
1831 in Nedvědice No. 24;[256] married (1) circa 1855, **Františka Moravcova**,
and (2) on 21 May 1867 in the village Velká Chýška in southern Bohemia,
Johanna Moravcova.[257] Františka, born 03 December 1831, and Johanna,
born 02 April 1834, were sisters, both born in the house in Velká Chýška No.
2, the daughters of Josef Moravec and Johanna Matoušová.[258] Františka died on

03 September 1866 and Joanna in 1882,[259] both deaths probably occurred in Velká Chýška. Karel and Františka were parents to six children:[260]

23   i.   Karolina[6] Příhodova, born 23 September 1855 in Velká Chýška No. 2. [At birth, Karolina was not a ligament child, but later Karel Příhoda declared that he was the father.]

24   ii.   Sofie (or Lofichka) Příhodova, born 07 June 1857 in Velká Chýška No. 15.

+   25   iii.   Jan Příhoda, born 31 May 1859, in Velká Chýška No. 25; died 22 November 1939 in Czechoslovakia; married 21 February 1881 in Pilsen, Bohemia, Karolina Kresslova.

26   iv.   Karel {Boromeus} Příhoda, born 08 September 1861, in Velká Chýška No. 25; married 04 July 1908 in Prague (the part Královské Vinohrady) to Marie Vorličková.

27   v.   Petr Pavel Příhoda, born 07 September 1863, in Velká Chýška No. 54; died 07 September 1866, in Velká Chýška No. 54.

28   vi.   Johanna Příhodova, born 24 April 1865, in Velká Chýška No. 54.

Karel and Johanna were parents to four children:[261]

+   29   vii.   Bedrick; (Bedřich; Frederick) Příhoda, born 25 November 1867 in Velká Chýška No. 54; died 01 January 1948 in Michigan City, La Porte County, Indiana; married 04 June 1888 in Chicago, Cook County, Illinois, Marie Balvin.

30   viii.   Theodor {Dorik} Příhoda, born 26 October 1870 in Velká Chýška No. 54; [died "in the trenches" during World War I, according to family lore] died 03 April 1916 in Prague III, in the area of parish P. Marie Vitězná.[262]

31   ix.   Maxmillian Příhoda, born 08 October 1872 in Velká Chýška No. 25; died 21 November 1872.

+   32   x.   Matylda Příhodova, born 15 March 1875 in Velká Chýška No. 25; baptized 16 March 1875 in Velká Chýška; died 09 March 1947 at 153 Fairmont Avenue, Maywood, New Jersey; buried 12 March 1947 in the New York Cemetery (now called Maple Grove Park Cemetery) in Hackensack, Bergen County, New Jersey; married 03 July 1904 in the Borough of Manhattan in New York City, New York, Adolf Rücker.

According to a Bible record kept by Matylda Příhodova, her father, Karel, married a third time.[263] This third wife has been identified from the christening records of Velká Chýška as Wilhelmina Konečná, a teacher from Hořepnik No. 80 and the daughter of Antonin Konečny.[264] Wilhelmina bore Karel's eleventh child:

> 33　xi.　Marie Apolena Příhodova, born 09 February 1888 in Velká Chýška No. 2.

25. Jan[6] Příhoda (Karel[5], Jan[4], Martin[3], Andreas[2], Jan[1]) born 31 May 1859 in Velká Chýška No. 25;[265] died 22 November 1939 in Czechoslovakia;[266] married 21 February 1881 in Pilsen, Bohemia, **Karolina Kresslova**, born 04 July 1863 in Bukova No. 45, Blathna District, Bohemia, the daughter of Marie Kresl; died 30 July 1938. Jan and Karolina raised a family of six children:[267]

> 34　i.　Frank[7] Příhoda, born circa 1882 in Pilsen, Bohemia; died circa 1882 in Pilsen from diphtheria.
>
> 35　ii.　Karlicka Příhodova, born in Pilsen and there died early from diphtheria.
>
> 36　iii.　Sofie Příhodova.
>
> 37　iv.　Wilhelma Příhodova, married a man known today only as Mr. Maier and with him had a daughter, Marketa.[268] Marketa married a man known only as Mr. Svoboda and with him had two sons. According to family lore, during World War II, these sons escaped from the Nazis to either Norway or Sweden, where today, they are engaged in engineering and architecture.[269]
>
> 38　v.　Ruzena ("Rose") Příhodova.
>
> +　39　vi.　Marie Příhodova, born 07 December 1888 in Prague; died 10 April 1969 in Prague; married in Prague, Karel Mašek.

29. Bedřich[6] (Bedrick; Frederick) **Příhoda** (Karel[5], Jan[4], Martin[3], Andreas[2], Jan[1]), born 25 November 1867 in Velká Chýška No. 54, Bohemia;[270] died 01 January 1948 in Michigan City, La Porte County, Indiana; buried 03 January 1948 in the Greenwood Cemetery, Michigan City;[271] married 04 June 1888 in Chicago, Cook County, Illinois, **Marie Balvin**,[272] born 02 February 1866 in Pilsen, Bohemia, the daughter of Joseph Balvin; died 09 April 1934 at 1619 West Eighth Street, Michigan City; buried 12 April 1934 in Michigan City.[273] At the time of the birth of their third child in 1895, Bedrick and Marie resided at "20th & Sangamon" in Chicago.[274] In the 1900 census, the family residence was recorded on West Eighteenth Place in Chicago and there were four children in the household. It also states in the 1900 census that Bedrick was a locksmith and came to America in 1890 and that Maria came in 1885.[275] (Efforts to locate the family in the 1910 census have been unsuccessful.[276]) In 1920, the family is found renting a house at 220 Logan Street in Michigan City, La Porte County, Indiana.[277] And according to the federal census of that year, Bedrick (recorded as "Fred") and Marie (recorded as "Mary") both immigrated to America in 1885. Bedrick indicated that he had filed his declaration to become a U.S. citizen, *i.e.*, his "First Papers;" Mary was listed as an alien. The following information regarding the birth dates of the four children of Bedrick and Marie comes from family Bible records. Confirmation from official birth certificates, has been located only for Jerome.[278,279]

+   40   i.   Jennie[7] M. Prihoda, born 10 November 1889 in Chicago, Cook County, Illinois; married 28 April 1913 in Chicago, George Kripner.

+   41   ii.   Charles Prihoda, born 01 June 1892 in Chicago; died March 1973 in Michigan City, La Porte County, Indiana; married Mary Malicka.

+   42   iii.   Jerome {Jaroslav} Prihoda, born 16 July 1895 in Chicago; died June 1971 in Michigan City; married Leona (née Barnett) Law.

     43   iv.   Peter Prihoda, born 02 November 1898 in Chicago; died 24 July 1959. Peter never married.[280]

32. Matylda[6] Přihodova (Karel[5], Jan[4], Martin[3], Andreas[2], Jan[1]), born 15 March 1875 in Velká Chýška; baptized 16 March 1875 in Velká Chýška;[281] died 09 March 1947 at 153 Fairmont Avenue, Maywood, New Jersey; buried 12 March 1947 in the New York Cemetery (now called the Maple Grove Park Cemetery) in Hackensack, Bergen County, New Jersey;[282] married 03 July 1904 in the Borough of Manhattan in New York City, New York, **Adolf Rücker**,[283] born 23 October 1876 in Horaždovic, Bohemia;[284,285] died 02 June 1938 at the family home at 135 Washington Avenue, Little Ferry, Bergen County, New Jersey; buried 08 June 1938 in the New York Cemetery.[286] Adolf and Matylda were parents to six children, five of whom survived to adulthood.[287]

+   44   i.   Carolina[7] Rucker, born 17 January 1906 at 52 Garden Street, Little Ferry; christened 29 April 1906 at the Church of the Immaculate Conception in Hackensack; died 27 July 1962 in Ridgewood, Bergen County, New Jersey; buried 30 July 1962 in the George Washington Memorial Park Cemetery, Paramus, Bergen County, New Jersey; married 24 July 1927 at the Church of the Immaculate Conception, Rudolph Komarek.

+   45   ii.   Mary Rucker, born 21 January 1907 at 135 Washington Avenue, Little Ferry; christened 02 August 1908 at the Church of the Immaculate Conception in Hackensack; married 09 July 1929 in Newport, Campbell County, Kentucky, William Franklin Frotscher.

+   46   iii.   Frances Rucker, born 04 April 1908 at 135 Washington Avenue, Little Ferry; christened 02 August 1908 at the Church of the Immaculate Conception in Hackensack; married 02 August 1931 at the Evangelical Congregational Church in Little Ferry, Floyd Skelton.

47   iv.   Edward Rucker, born 01 August 1909 at 135 Washington Avenue, Little Ferry;[288] served in the U.S. Army during World War II.[289] Currently resides at the family home at 135 Washington Avenue, Little Ferry, New Jersey.

48   v.   Adolph Rucker, born 22 December 1910 at 135 Washington Avenue, Little Ferry;[290] served in the U.S. Army during World War II. Currently resides at the family home at 135 Washington Avenue, Little Ferry, New Jersey.

49   vi.   Matylda Rucker born 15 March 1917 at 135 Washington Avenue, Little Ferry; died 05 April 1917; buried 09 April 1917 in the New York Cemetery in Hackensack.[291]

39. Marie[7] Příhodova (Jan[6], Karel[5], Jan[4], Martin[3], Andreas[2], Jan[1]), born 07 December 1888 in Prague; died 10 April 1969 in Prague; married in Prague, **Karel Mašek**, born 11 February 1885 in Prague, the son of Thomáš Mašek and Marie Vaňková; died 16 October 1965 in Prague. Marie and Karel were parents to eight children, all born in Prague.[292]

50   i.   Hermína[8] Mašek born 24 November 1911, married Adolfa Kotapiše.

51   ii.   Marie Mašek born 20 June 1913; died May 1990; married (1) Mr. Napomuckaho; (2) Josefa Brycha.

52   iii.   Věra Mašek born 03 December 1914; died 10 May 1958; married Václava Nováka.

53   iv.   Karel Mašek born 10 June 1919; died 26 June 1990; married (1) Kvela Mastaková; (2) Dana Kopecká. Karel was the father to three children: Thomáš, Dana, and Karel.

54   v.   Jiří Mašek born 02 March 1921; married Irena Kokštejnová. Jiří and Irena were parents to three sons: Jiří, Jan, and Josef.

+   55   vi.   Joseph {Josef} Mašek born 10 May 1922; married (1) Jeanne (née Nadeau) Desjardins; (2) Micheline Marie-Anna Mallet.

56   vii.   Libuše Mašek born 29 June 1923; married Mr. Navrátila.

+   57   viii.   Jaroslav Mašek born 22 August 1925; married Marie Macelová.

40. Jennie[7] M. Prihoda (Bedřich[6], Karel[5], Jan[4], Martin[3], Andreas[2], Jan[1]), born 10 November 1889 in Chicago, Cook County, Illinois; died 01 February 1968 at St. Anthony de Padua Hospital in Chicago; buried 03 February 1968 in the National Bohemian Cemetery in Chicago; married 28 April 1913 at 1510 West Eighteenth Street, Chicago, **George Kripner**,[293] born circa 1887 in Illinois. (George's parents both were born in Bohemia.) In 1920, the family resided at 1615 South Karlov Avenue in Chicago, property which they rented. At the time of Jennie's death in 1968, her residence was still listed as 1615 South Karlov Avenue. Jennie and George had at least four children, all born in Illinois, probably in Chicago.[294]

58   i.   Frederick[8] Kripner born February 1914.

59   ii.   Emily Kripner born May 1915; married and relocated with her family to California.[295]

60   iii.   George Kripner born March 1917.

61   iv.   Jerome ("Gerald") Kripner born 29 August 1918; died 26 October 1983 at the Palos Community Hospital in Palos Heights, Illinois.[296] During his life, he had been married and earned his living as a pipe fitter. He was buried on 29 October 1983 in the Evergreen Cemetery, Evergreen Park, Illinois.[297]

41. Charles[7] Prihoda (Bedřich[6], Karel[5], Jan[4], Martin[3], Andreas[2], Jan[1]), born 01 June 1892 in Chicago, Cook County, Illinois; died 30 March 1973 at 315 Greenwood Avenue, Michigan City, La Porte County, Indiana;[298] buried 02 April 1973 in the Greenwood Cemetery in Michigan City; married **Mary Malicka**,[299] born 19 December 1898 in Prague, Bohemia, Austrian

Empire, the daughter of August and Marketa Malicka; died 20 March 1989 in St. Anthony Hospital in Michigan City; buried 22 March 1989 in Greenwood Cemetery. Charles had been the maintenance supervisor for the Excelsior Cycle Company. At the time of her death, Mary resided in the family home at 2410 Oak Street in Michigan City.[300] At the time of her marriage to Charles, Mary was a widow with children.[301] Today, her daughter, , Georgia (née Law) Utpatel lives with her husband, Arthur G. Utpatel, at the family home at 2410 Oak Street. Charles and Mary had no children.[302]

42. Jerome[7] {Jaroslav} Prihoda (Bedřich[6], Karel[5], Jan[4], Martin[3], Andreas[2], Jan[1]), born 16 July 1895 in Chicago, Cook County, Illinois; died 07 June 1971 in St. Anthony Hospital in Michigan City, La Porte County, Indiana; buried 09 June 1971 in Greenwood Cemetery, Michigan City;[303] married **Leona (née Barnett) Law**, born 30 July 1900, the daughter of Seldon James Barnett and Maude Fryemire; died 25 February 1976 in Michigan City;[304] buried 28 February 1976 in Greenwood Cemetery.[305] Leona had two children with her first husband, Mr. Law: Keith Law and Frances (née Law) Smith.[306] (Frances married Grant Smith.) Jerome served in the U.S. Army during World War I[307] and later worked as an inspector for Weil-McLain. A the time of his death, both Jerome and Leona lived at 1619 West Eighth Street in Michigan City. Jerome and Leona had no children.[308]

44. Carolina[7] ("Carrie") Rucker (Matylda (née Příhodova)[6], Karel[5], Jan[4], Martin[3], Andreas[2], Jan[1]), born 17 January 1906 at 52 Garden Street, Little Ferry, Bergen County, New Jersey; christened 29 April 1906 at the Church of the Immaculate Conception in Hackensack, Bergen County, New Jersey;[309] died 27 July 1962 in Ridgewood, Bergen County, New Jersey; buried 30 July 1962 in the George Washington Memorial Park Cemetery, Paramus, Bergen County, New Jersey;[310,311] married 24 July 1927 at St Margaret's Church in Little Ferry,[312] **Rudolph Komarek**,[313] born 05 October 1903 in Krompach, Bohemia,[314] the son of Rudolph Komarek and Anna Thua (or Thui);[315] died 20 February 1987 at the Humana Hospital in Louisville, Jefferson County, Kentucky; buried 23 February 1987 in George Washington Memorial Park Cemetery.[316] Carrie and Rudolph were parents to two sons:

62	i.	Rudolph[8] Arthur Komarek, born 11 November 1929 in the Hackensack Hospital, Hackensack, Bergen County, New Jersey.[317]
+ 63	ii.	Robert Edwin Komarek, born 07 October 1932 in the Hackensack Hospital; married 17 September 1955 in Ridgewood, Bergen County, New Jersey, Sally Ann French.

45. Mary[7] **Rucker** (Matylda (née Příhodova)[6], Karel[5], Jan[4], Martin[3], Andreas[2], Jan[1]), born 21 January 1907 at 135 Washington Avenue, Little Ferry, Bergen County, New Jersey; christened 02 August 1908 at the Church of the Immaculate Conception in Hackensack, Bergen County, New Jersey;[318] married 09 July 1929 in Newport, Campbell County, Kentucky, **William Franklin Frotscher**,[319] born 11 October 1903 in Bellevue, Campbell County, Kentucky, the son of Herman C. Frotscher, born 1858 in Germany, and Elizabeth Barteswelt, born 1866 in Germany;[320,321] died 27 January 1990 in Chambersburg Hospital, Chambersburg, Franklin County, Pennsylvania; remains cremated 28 January 1990 by the Smithsburg Crematory, Smithsburg, Washington County, Maryland.[322]

+   64   i.   William[8] Franklin Frotscher, Jr., born 12 January 1934 in the Hackensack Hospital, Hackensack, Bergen County, New Jersey; married (1) 01 August 1959 in Chester, Delaware County, Pennsylvania, Cherry Aurelia (née Winford) Cooper; (2) 20 August 1988 in Newburg, Cumberland County, Pennsylvania, Sarah Ann (née Hamilton) Buttermore.

46. Frances[7] **Rucker** (Matylda (née Příhodova)[6], Karel[5], Jan[4], Martin[3], Andreas[2], Jan[1]), born 04 April 1908 at 135 Washington Avenue, Little Ferry, Bergen County, New Jersey;[323] christened 02 August 1908 at the Church of the Immaculate Conception in Hackensack, Bergen County, New Jersey;[324] married 02 August 1931 at the Evangelical Congregational Church in Little Ferry, **Floyd Skelton**,[325] born 03 September 1904 at his parents home, 302 Dayton Avenue, Dayton, Campbell County, Kentucky, the son of Isaac Franklin Skelton and Augusta Dieterle;[326,327] died 18 October 1982 at his home, 215 Shippensburg Road, Shippensburg, Cumberland County, Pennsylvania; remains cremated 20 October 1982 by East Harrisburg Crematory, Harrisburg, Dauphin County, Pennsylvania.[328]

+   65   i.   Earl[8] Franklin Skelton, born 08 April 1940 in the Hackensack Hospital, Hackensack, Bergen County, New Jersey; married (1) 17 June 1962 in Hackensack, Anita Patton; (2) 17 November 1989 in Washington, DC, Thelma Francesca (Francine) (née Fried) Rudich.

55. Joseph[8] {Josef} **Mašek** (Marie[7] (née Příhodova), Jan[6], Karel[5], Jan[4], Martin[3], Andreas[2], Jan[1]), born 10 May 1922 in Prague; married (1) in Montreal, Quebec Province, Canada, **Jeanne (née Nadeau) Desjardins**, born 28 July 1921 in Rock Island, Quebec Province; married (2) in Montreal, **Micheline Marie-Anna Mallet**, born, the first of eleven children, of Omer George Mallet, a ship builder, and Marie-Anna LeBouthilier of Centre St. Simon, New Brunswick Province, Canada. Joseph and Jeanne had a son:[329]

66   i.   Jan[9] Mašek, born 14 April 1952 in Montreal.

Josef and Michelle are parents to two children:[330]

67   ii.   Barbara Marie Anna Masek, born 29 November 1962 at St. Mary's Hospital in San Francisco, California;[331] married Kenneth Henley. Barbara and Kenneth have a daughter, Sarah-Marie Anna Henley, born 26 November 1995.

68   iii.   Marc Masek, born 26 September 1965 at Kaiser Foundation Hospital in San Francisco;[332] married Eva —?—, born in Puerto Vallarta, Mexico. Marc and Eva have a son, Andrew Masek, born 01 May 1996.

57. Jaroslav[8] Mašek (Marie[7] (née Přihodova), Jan[6], Karel[5], Jan[4], Martin[3], Andreas[2], Jan[1]), born 22 August 1925 in Prague; married 20 October 1950, **Marie Macelová**, born 26 October 1926. Jaroslav and Marie reared two children:[333]

69   i.   Jana[9] Mašek, born 22 January 1953; married 22 October 1975 Ladislava Zemana.

70   ii.   Jaroslava Mašek, born 18 May 1967.

63. Robert[8] Edwin Komarek (Carolina (née Rucker)[7], Matylda (née Přihodova)[6], Karel[5], Jan[4], Martin[3], Andreas[2], Jan[1]), born 07 October 1932 in the Hackensack Hospital, Hackensack, Bergen County, New Jersey;[334] married 17 September 1955 in Christ Church in Ridgewood, Bergen County, New Jersey,[335] **Sally Ann French**, born 01 April 1933 in Passaic, Passaic County, New Jersey, the daughter of Joseph L. Paul French and Edith Mae Spjit.[336] Robert and Sally are the parents of two children, both born in The Valley Hospital, in Ridgewood:

71   i.   Bonnie[9] Jean Komarek, born 02 December 1957 at The Valley Hospital, Ridgewood, Bergen County, New Jersey;[337] married 04 January 1992 at The Church by the Sea in Madeira Beach, Pinellas County, Florida, John F. Hall, born 27 August 1953 in Maryland.[338] Bonnie and John have a son, Ryan Samuel Hall, born 27 June 1995 in Glendale Heights, Du Page County, Illinois.[339] A second son, Patrick, was added to the family in the fall of 1997.

72   ii.   Robert John Komarek, born 18 July 1959 at The Valley Hospital, Ridgewood, Bergen County, New Jersey;[340] married 23 December 1985 in Ponce, Puerto Rico, Maria Falcon.[341]

64. William[8] Franklin Frotscher, Junior (Mary (née Rucker)[7], Matylda (née Příhodova)[6], Karel[5], Jan[4], Martin[3], Andreas[2], Jan[1]), born 12 January 1934 in the Hackensack Hospital, Hackensack, Bergen County, New Jersey;[342] married (1) 01 August 1959 in Chester, Delaware County, Pennsylvania, **Cherry Aurelia (née Winford) Cooper**,[343] born 20 February 1936 in St. Paul, Ramsey County, Minnesota; the daughter of Orion P. Winford and Margaret E. Wharry of 1600 East River Boulevard, Minneapolis, Minnesota;[344] raised by her mother and step-father, Clarence Cooper; married (2) 20 August 1988 in Newburg, Cumberland County, Pennsylvania, **Sarah Ann (née Hamilton) Buttermore**, born 26 June 1945 in Fort Benning, Chattahoochee County, Georgia.[345,346] William and Cherry are/were parents to five children:

73   i.   Susan[9] Frances Frotscher, born 22 May 1963 in Waynesboro, Franklin County, Pennsylvania; married (1) 17 August 1985 in the Woolrich United Methodist Church in Woolrich, Clinton County, Pennsylvania, Jeffrey Goodman Collson, born 11 July 1962 in Elmira, Chemung County, New York; married (2) 30 April 1994 in the New Hope United Methodist Church in Newburg, Cumberland County, Pennsylvania, Lance William Heberlig, born 20 Jun 1961 in Chambersburg, Franklin County, Pennsylvania, the son of William George Heberlig and Judith (née Plank) Heberlig.[347] Susan and Jeffrey were divorced on 09 December 1993[348] and had no children. Susan and Lance are parents to a son, William Franklin Heberlig, born 16 June 1997 at the Carlisle Hospital, Carlisle, Cumberland County, Pennsylvania.[349]

74   ii.   William Franklin Frotscher III, born 08 February 1968 in Gettysburg, Adams County, Pennsylvania; died 09 May 1970 in Chambersburg Hospital, Chambersburg, Franklin County, Pennsylvania; remains cremated 12 May 1970 by the East Harrisburg Crematory, Harrisburg, Dauphin County, Pennsylvania.[350]

75   iii.   David Daniel Frotscher, born 18 October 1971 in Williamsport, Lycoming County, Pennsylvania (adopted).

76   iv.   Jennifer Frotscher, born 10 February 1973 in the Republic of South Korea (adopted); died 28 June 1977 at the M. S. Hershey Medical Center, Hershey, Dauphin County, Pennsylvania; remains cremated 29 June 1973 by the East Harrisburg Crematory, Harrisburg, Dauphin County, Pennsylvania.[351]

77   v.   Lynelle Jean Frotscher, born 01 August 1974 in the Republic of South Korea (adopted); married Todd Matthew Kilgore, born circa 1973, the son of Joseph Kilgore.[352] Lynelle and Todd are parents to three children, all born in Chambersburg: Matthew Kilgore, born 08 February 1993; Jessica Marie Kilgore, born 22 February 1995; and a daughter born 10 January 1997.[353]

65. Earl[8] Franklin Skelton (Frances (née Rucker)[7], Matylda (née Příhodova)[6], Karel[5], Jan[4], Martin[3], Andreas[2], Jan[1]), born 08 April 1940 in the Hackensack Hospital, Hackensack, Bergen County, New Jersey;[354] married (1) 17 June 1962 in Hackensack, **Anita Patton**,[355] born 09 July 1940 at the Beth El Hospital in Brooklyn, New York City, New York, the daughter of Kenneth Grayson Patton and Gertrude Feldrais;[356] divorced 14 February 1986 in Washington, DC;[357] (2) 19 October 1986 in Washington, DC, **Thelma Francesca (née Fried) Rudich**,[358] born 17 November 1939 at the Jewish Maternity Hospital in Manhattan, New York City, New York, the daughter of Albert Fried and Mary Diamond.[359] Earl and Anita are parents to two children:

78   i.   Diane[9] Lynne Skelton, born 23 September 1965 at the Samaritan Hospital in Troy, Rensselaer County, New York;[360] married 24 June 1989 in Cox, Midi-Pyrenees, France and again 20 August 1989 in Washington, DC[361], Patrice Yves Faujour, born 06 December 1957 in Nantes, Loire-Atlantique, France, the son of Claude Yves Faujour and Therese Henriette Augereau.[362] Diane, later called Diana, and Patrice are the parents of two daughters: Joline Mariya Faujour, born 31 January 1991 at the Holy Cross Hospital, Silver Spring, Montgomery County, Maryland;[363] and Delora Kathline Faujour, born 07 December 1993 in Melun, Seine-et-Marne, France.[364]

79   ii.   Isaac Patton Skelton,[365,366] born 11 November 1971 at the Columbia Hospital for Women in Washington, DC;[367] married 21 October 1996 in City Hall, Manhattan, New York City, New York,[368] Dana Segal Sevastyanova, born 18 May 1973 in Donetsk, Ukraine, Russia, USSR, the daughter of Vladimir Sevastyanov and Lea Segal.[369] On 22 September 1997 in New York, Isaac and Dana became the parents of a daughter, Dora Segal Skelton.[370]

Epilogue

The pages preceding this are history. On those leaves, our factual knowledge of past events of our family and of their actions have been chronicled. Hopefully they have allowed you, the reader, to paint a mental image of past events and the people who lived them. It is hoped that you may have developed a deeper sense of family bonds and come to realize that some of the characteristics that we each possess, may have been passed down to us by our forebears.

We can record the past, but we cannot change it. It is immutable. We should realize that the future is more important. We can learn from mistakes of our ancestors and build upon and be inspired by their life's works. Many of their lives were hard, others may appear to have been superficially nonproductive — but they all contributed — and more than just their genes to us. They contributed attitudes and motivators which have been passed down through the generations and, knowingly or unknowingly, make us what we are today. It is this realization to which we should become aware and therefore do all that we can to help our children, and their children, and thereby help future generations of our family.

Two things a parent must give a child: One is wings... — *the other is roots.*

E. F. S.

INDEX

Surnames are indexed under their simplest form, *e.g.*, Rücker is indexed under "Rucker"; Příhoda, Příhodova, and Prihodova are all indexed under "Prihoda."

Females are referenced under their maiden and all married surnames.

Localities are indexed under the country, state, county, or province.

Cemeteries, churches, colleges and universities are indexed under both their formal names and the categories "cemeteries," "churches," and "colleges and universities," respectively.

Indexing topics are referenced under the following categories:

Family stories, letters, mementos, and so forth are consolidated under "Family lore and Memorabilia."

Endnotes

[1]Joseph Ward Swain, *The Harper History of Civilization.* [New York, NY: Harper and Bros., Pub., 1958], Vol. I, p. 334.

[2]*Czechoslovakia, A Country Study.* (Washington, DC: U.S. Government Printing Office, 1989), 3.

[3]David W. Paul, *Czechoslovakia Profile of a Socialist Republic at the Crossroads of Europe.* [Boulder, CO: Westview Press, 1982), 4-6.

[4]Lonnie R. Johnson, *Central Europe Enemies, Neighbors, Friends.* (New York, NY: Oxford University Press, 1996), 64-68.

[5]*Czechoslovakia, A Country Study*, 3.

[6]L. R. Johnson, 87-90.

[7]Frederick G. Heymann, *Poland & Czechoslovakia.* (Englewood Cliffs, NJ: Prentice-Hall, Inc., 1966), 105.

[8]"Mittel-Östliches Deutschland oder Böhman, Mähren und Schlesien" Originally published in 1822; rev. 1844; reproduced by Jonathan Sheppard Books, Albany, NY as "(M 8) The East Central Provinces: Bohemia, Moravia and Silesia - 1844. This 1844 map shows the area east of Bavaria and Saxony and west of Crackow." [RP0004]

[9]Complete details of the invasion known today as "Prague Spring," are given in the following work: Philip Windson and Adam Roberts, *Czechoslovakia 1968 Reform, Repression and Resistance.* (New York, NY: Columbia University Press, 1969).

[10]"A Thousand Years of Czech Culture," in *Winston-Salem Journal.* (Winston-Salem, NC, 1996-1997).

[11]Kartografie Praha, "Jižni Chesy, prûvodce regionem," 1997.

[12]Citations to the sources for all genealogical records are given in the section entitled "Genealogical Summary: Descendants of Ignaz Rücker and Josefa Veselá"

[13]State District Archive (herein after cited as "SDA") Pilzeň Alphabetical Register of Records from the City Hall in Horažd'ovice.

[14]Letter from Mr. David Kohout dated 13 May 1998 to the author; hereinafter cited as "Letter from David Kohout; 13 May 1998.". Mr. Kohout, a professional genealogist living at Janáčkovo nábřeži 57, 150 00 Praha 5, Czech Republic, Europe was commissioned by the author in 1997 and 1998 to research the Rücker and Prihoda families. All the Czech records cited in this work were uncovered by Mr. Kohout.

The information about the descendants of Tomáž Rücker and Josefa (née Protivová) Rückerová was obtained by Mr. Kohout from Marie (née Nová) Rückerová, widow of the late Václav Rücker (1930-1991). (Her present address and that of her brother-in-law, Jaroslav Rücker, are given in the Endnotes attached to the Genealogical Summary of the Rücker family (#133 & #134).)

[15]1900 U.S. Census (population), New Jersey, Bergen Co., Lodi Twp., Little Ferry Borough, Super. Dist. 3; Enum. Dist. 25, p. 3, dwell. 32; fam. 38; National Archives Microfilm Publication T623, Roll 955.

[16]1910 U.S. Census (population), New Jersey, Bergen Co., Lodi Twp., Little Ferry Borough, Super. Dist. 178; Enum. Dist. 31, p. 22A, dwell. 363; visit. 408; National Archives Microfilm Publication T624, Roll 869.

[17]1920 U.S. Census (population), New Jersey, Bergen Co., Little Ferry Borough, Super. Dist. 6; Enum. Dist. 38, p. 21B, dwell. 335; visit. 449; National Archives Microfilm Publication T625, Roll 1018.

[18]*History of Bergen County New Jersey 1630 - 1923*, Frances E. Westervelt, ed. (New York, NY: Lewis

Historical Publishing Co., Inc., 1923), 375.

[19]Bergen Co., NJ Deed Book **391**, 444-446. The lot locations are identified on Bergen County Map No. 492, *Map of Property of Victor Marschall [sic.] at Little Ferry N.J.*

[20]Untitled pamphlet about the history of Little Ferry, NJ; available at Little Ferry Public Library, 239 Liberty St., Little Ferry, NJ 07643.

[21]"Discharged Employee Kills Girl at Little Ferry, Shoots at Her Sister and Ends His Own Life," *The Bergen News*, 06 May 1912, p. 1, on Bergen News Microfilm Vol. 1, 06 Feb. 1912 - 29 June 1912.

[22]1920 U.S. Census (population), New Jersey, Bergen Co., Little Ferry Borough, Super. Dist. 6; Enum. Dist. 38, p. 21B, dwell. 335; visit. 449; National Archives Microfilm Publication T625, Roll 1018.

[23]Memorandum dated 15 May 1997 to the author from Mr. Mark Tomko, Asst. Chief Clerk, Office of the Bergen County Clerk, Hackensack, NJ, in which it is stated: "Please be advised that a search of our records provide no information on Karel Rucker." [RP020]

[24]Bergen County Deed Books **411**, 557 (1894); **520**, 240 (1901); **526**, 396 (1901); **552**, 530 (1902); **586**, 229 (1904); **604**, 184 (1905); **611**, 567 (1905); **623**, 297 (1906); **624**, 250 (1906); **633**, 267 (1906); **633**, 371 (1906); and **725**, 199 (1909).

[25]1900 U.S. Census (population), New Jersey, Bergen Co., Lodi Twp., Little Ferry Borough, Super. Dist. 3; Enum. Dist. 25, p. 3, dwell. 32; fam. 38; National Archives Microfilm Publication T623, Roll 955.

[26]1900 U.S. Census (population), New Jersey, Bergen Co., Lodi Twp., Little Ferry Borough, Super. Dist. 3; Enum. Dist. 25, p. 3, dwell. 33; fam. 39; National Archives Microfilm Publication T623, Roll 955.

[27]Bergen Co. Mortgage Book **136**, 88 (26 Jun. 1901).

[28]Baptismal Register, Church of the Immaculate Conception, 49 Vreeland Ave., Hackensack, NJ, Vol. I, p. 46, No. 965.

[29]Taped interview on 10 May 1997 with Mary (née Rucker) Frotscher and Frances (née Rucker) Skelton at the home of Mary Frotscher at 30 Pine Tree Lane, Newburg, PA 17240-9381.

[30]Bergen Co. Deed Book **1473**, 15, 17, 19, 22, 24, and 26; each dated 30 Dec. 1926 and recorded 19 Jan. 1927.

[31]Bergen County, NJ Will Book 187, p. 163 (Docket 34, p. 120, #66,478).

[32]*The Bergen Evening Record*, Monday, 07 April 1947, p. 2; *The Bergen Evening Record* Microfilm Roll No. 202: 05 Apr. 1949 thru 10 June 1947; Johnson Free Public Library, 274 Main St., Hackensack, NJ 07601.

[33]1910 U.S. Census (population), New Jersey, Bergen Co., Lodi Twp., Little Ferry Borough, Super. Dist. 178; Enum. Dist. 31, p. 22A, dwell. 363; visit. 408; National Archives Microfilm Publication T624, Roll 869.

[34]There is little doubt that this is the handwriting of Adolf Rücker. It matches his signature on his Certificate of Naturalization. (See Fig. II-4.)

[35]*Passenger and Crew Lists of Vessels Arriving at New Yokr, NY — April 27 - 29, 1903*, Vol. 601-602, List K, p. 159, line 19; National Archives Microfilm Publication T715, Roll 348.

[36]Czech Marriage Certificate of Adolf Rücker and Matylda Prihoda. The certificate is framed and stored in the family home at 135 Washington Avenue, Little Ferry, NJ. Except for a footnote, the entire certificate is written in Czech. It was translated on Saturday, 04 November 1995 by Frances (née Rucker) Skelton and her grandson, Isaac Patton Skelton. The English footnote says the following: "Vydal Rev. Vincent Pesek,

V. D., 347 East 74th St., New York, NYC."

[37]Declaration of Intention No. 595, filed 31 Mar. 1910 at the Bergen County, NJ Court House in Hackensack, NJ.

[38]Bergen Co., NJ, Immigration and Naturalization Records, Vol. 7, No. 1669, issued 23 June 1916.

[39]Untitled pamphlet about the history of Little Ferry, NJ; op. cit.

[40]A copy of the World War I draft registration card of Adolf Rücker was obtained from the National Archives - Southeast Region, 1557 St. Joseph Avenue, East Point, GA 30344-2593. [RP005]

[41]Maple Grove Park Cemetery records, op. cit.

[42]1920 U.S. Census (population), New Jersey, Bergen Co., Little Ferry Borough, Super. Dist. 6; Enum. Dist. 38, p. 21B, dwell. 333; visit. 444; National Archives Microfilm Publication T625, Roll 1018.

[43]World War I draft registration card of Adolf Rücker, op cit.

[44]1910 U.S. Census (population), New Jersey, Bergen Co., Lodi Twp., Little Ferry Borough, Super. Dist. 178; Enum. Dist. 31, p. 22A, dwell. 364; visit. 409; National Archives Microfilm Publication T624, Roll 869.,

[45]Bergen Co., NJ, Immigration and Naturalization Records, Vol. 7, No. 1669, issued 23 June 1916.

[46]1910 U.S. Census (population), New Jersey, Bergen Co., Lodi Twp., Little Ferry Borough, Super. Dist. 178; Enum. Dist. 31, p. 22A, dwell. 364; visit. 409; National Archives Microfilm Publication T624, Roll 869.

[47]Letter from David Kohout; 13 May 1998, op. cit.

[48]Ibid.

[49](1) "Kills Girl of 17 as She Tries to Aid Him," New York Times, 06 May 1912, p. 26 on "The New York Times" Microfilm Roll 474, 1-15 May 1912; (2) "Discharged Employee Kills Girl at Little Ferry, Shoots at Her Sister and Ends His Own Life," The Bergen News, 06 May 1912, p. 1, on "Bergen News" Microfilm Vol. 1, 06 Feb. 1912 - 29 June 1912; (3) "Murder and Suicide," The Hackensack Republican, 09 May 1912, p. 8, on "The Hackensack Republican" Microfilm, Roll 17, 04 Jan. 1912 - 12 Jun. 1913. Each of these microfilm records was viewed at the Johnson Free Public Library, op. cit..

[50]There is a discrepancy as to whose house was hit by the bullet fired at Carrie Rucker. According to the article in "The New York Times," the bullet "...crashed through the parlor window in Orrin Peter's house across the street and Mr. Peter's face was cut by the flying glass." According to the Bergen News, "...the bullet missed her [Carrie], went through the glass in the door, crashed through a window in the apartment of Mrs. John Dare at the opposite side of the street and embedded itself in the wall." In a conversation with Mary (née Rucker) Frotscher on 10 May 1997 at her home in Newburg, PA, she said that the stray bullet lodged in the Dare home.

[51]On 12 Nov. 1996, Charles A. Karkut, New Jersey State Registrar of Vital Statistics, signed the following statement: "This certifies that the original records and all appropriate indexes of this office have been carefully searched and no record found of the death of Anton/Anthony Parchal/Parchall on 5/5/12 or any day during 1912."

On 06 May 1997, the author also searched a portion of the aforementioned records at the New Jersey State Archives in Trenton with the same negative result.

[52]Bergen County Deed Book 16, 814 (24 May 1912).

[53]The Record, Thursday, 26 October 1967, p. D-10; The Record Microfilm Roll No. 780: 21 Oct. 1967 through 31 Oct. 1967; Johnson Free Public Library, op. cit..

[54]Confirmed by the Alumni Office of Tufts University by telephone on 05 August 1997.

[55]Bergen Co. Mortgage Book **2978**, 198 (08 Jul. 1954).

[56]Obituary, "Dr. W. Rucker Is Dead At 66," *The Sunday Record*, p. B-8 (02 Aug. 1970). [RP037]

[57]Letter from Mrs. Mary (née Rucker) Frotscher postmarked 17 June 1996 to the author; hereinafter referred to as "Letter from Mary Frotscher; 17 Jun. 1996."

[58]Wills of Bergen County, NJ, Docket 82, p. 164, No. M42,654.

[59]Obituary, "Dr. Vendela E. Olson, led lung association," *The Record*, p. A-10 (06 Mar. 1984). [RP037]

[60]Certificate of Death of Charles Rucker, Florida State File No. 80-070474; Local File No. 00137. [RP033]

[61]The current address for Carlton W. Rucker is 311 Sutton Avenue; Hackensack, New Jersey 07601.

[62]As previously noted, all Czech records reported in this genealogy were uncovered by Mr. David Kohout.

[63]SDA Pilzeň Czech Republic, Book 20 for Horažd'ovice Parish, pp. 51-52.

[64]SDA Pilzeň Register of the Parish records No. 25, Horažd'ovice Parish; see also the book of weddings No. 21 for the years 1794-1839.

[65]SDA Pilzeň Czech Republic, Book 20 for Horažd'ovice Parish, pp. 280-281.

[66]SDA Pilzeň Register of the Parish, Book No. 16, Horažd'ovice Parish; p. 552.

[67]*Ibid.*

[68]Mr. Kohout makes the following statement regarding the death record for Hynek (= Ignaz) Rücker: "In the archives [SDA] are the death records till the year 1890 and the alphabetic register of these records till the year 1896 /the younger are still on City Halls/. ... In the alphabetic register is the note: 'Hynek Rücker, died 2.6.1893 [= 02 June 1893]

in Horažd'ovice - the suburb, the No. of house 104 - see the page No. 44 of the parish book."

[69]SDA Pilzeň Czech Republic, Book 23 for Horažd'ovice Parish, p. 1.

[70]SDA Pilzeň Register of the Parish, Book No. 18, Horažd'ovice Parish; p. 33.

[71]SDA Pilzeň Register of the Parish, Book No. 28, Horažd'ovice Parish; p. 17.

[72]SDA Pilzeň Register of the Parish, Book No. 28, Horažd'ovice Parish.

[73]SDA Pilzeň Register of the Parish, Book No. 28, Horažd'ovice Parish.

[74]SDA Třeboň Parish Register, Bohumilice Parish, p. 66.

[75]Letter from David Kohout; 13 May 1998, *op. cit.*

[76]SDA Pilzeň Alphabetical Register of Records from the City Hall in Horažd'ovice.

[77]Letter from David Kohout; 13 May 1998, *op. cit.*

[78]SDA Pilzeň Alphabetical Register of Records from the City Hall in Horažd'ovice.

[79]Letter from David Kohout; 13 May 1998, *op. cit.*

[80]SDA Pilzeň Register of the Parish, Book No. 28, Horažd'ovice Parish; p. 17.

[81]Records of the Maple Grove Park Cemetery (formerly The New York Cemetery), 535 Hudson St., Hackensack, NJ; Lot Nos. 35 and 35N, Sect. E.

[82]1900 U.S. Census (population), New Jersey, Bergen Co., Lodi Twp., Little Ferry Borough, Super. Dist. 3; Enum. Dist. 25, p. 3, dwell. 32; fam. 38; National Archives Microfilm Publication T623, Roll 955.

1910 U.S. Census (population), New Jersey, Bergen Co., Lodi Twp., Little Ferry Borough, Super. Dist. 178; Enum. Dist. 31, p. 22A, dwell. 363; visit. 408; National Archives Microfilm Publication T624, Roll 869. Note: On her marriage record dated 25 November 1891 (cited below), Barbara's age is reported as 20; on the 1894 birth record of her daughter, Mary, (cited below), her age is given as 23; and in the 1910 census record (cited here), her age is reported as 39. All three records correspond to her birth in 1871; in the 1900 census (cited here), her birth month and year are given as October 1870.

[83]New Jersey State Archives; Marriage Records; Drawer 413; Place 42; Certif. R 52.

[84]Records of the Maple Grove Park Cemetery, *op. cit.*

[85]1900 U.S. Census (population), New Jersey, Bergen Co., Lodi Twp., Little Ferry Borough, Super. Dist. 3; Enum. Dist. 25, p. 3, dwell. 32; fam. 38; National Archives Microfilm Publication T623, Roll 955.
1910 U.S. Census (population), New Jersey, Bergen Co., Lodi Twp., Little Ferry Borough, Super. Dist. 178; Enum. Dist. 31, p. 22A, dwell. 363; visit. 408; National Archives Microfilm Publication T624, Roll 869.
1920 U.S. Census (population), New Jersey, Bergen Co., Little Ferry Borough, Super. Dist. 6; Enum. Dist. 38, p. 21B, dwell. 335; visit. 449; National Archives Microfilm Publication T625, Roll 1018.

[86]Birth Certificate of Mary Rucker (R33), NJ Dept. of Health and Senior Services. [RP002]

[87](1) "Kills Girl of 17 as She Tries to Aid Him," *New York Times*, 06 May 1912, p. 26 on "The New York Times" Microfilm Roll 474, 1-15 May 1912; (2) "Discharged Employee Kills Girl at Little Ferry, Shoots at Her Sister and Ends His Own Life," *The Bergen News*, 06 May 1912, p. 1, on "Bergen News" Microfilm Vol. 1, 06 Feb. 1912 - 29 June 1912; (3) "Murder and Suicide," *The Hackensack Republican*, 09 May 1912, p. 8, on "The Hackensack Republican" Microfilm, Roll 17, 04 Jan. 1912 - 12 Jun. 1913. Each of these microfilm records was

viewed at the Johnson Free Public Library, *op. cit..*

[88]Death Certificate of Carrie (née Rucker) Vaclavicek, No. 47319, NJ State Bureau of Vital Statistics. [RP021]

[89]Letter from Raymond J. Dohm, Representative of George Washington Memorial Park Cemetery, P. O. Box 21, Paramus & Cemetery Rds., Paramus, NJ 07652, post marked 19 July 1995, to the author; hereinafter cited as "Letter from R. J. Dohm; 19 Jul. 1995." [RP021]
[It is curious to note that circa 1960 in Bergen Co., NJ, Raymond J. Dohm married Linda Reder, older sister of Carol N. Reder who is referenced on pp. 129-130 of this work.]

[90]Marriage record of Charles Vaclavicek and Caroline Rucker; New Jersey State Archives; Marriage Records; 1918 Marriage Certificates; Vol. 33 (Tr-V); Microfilm Reel No. 10; Record No. 315. [RP021]

[91]Taped interview with Mary Frotscher and Frances Skelton on 10 May 1997, *op. cit.*

[92]*Automated Archives, Inc.* "Social Security Death Benefit Records 1937 through June 1991," M - Z; CD #112 (GRS 3.03; 1994). [RP035] Hereinafter cited as "Soc. Sec. Death Records."

[93]Todeserklaerung (Death Certificate) of Dr. William Charles Rucker, No. 5345; dated 29 Juli 1970; copy obtained from Standesamt, Landeshauptstadt, Heiligerstraße 1, 30159 Hannover, Germany. [RP037]

[94]Letter from R. J. Dohm; 19 Jul. 1995, *op. cit.*

[95]Obituary, *The Sunday Record*, p. B-8 (02 Aug. 1970). [RP037]

[96]Bergen Co. Wills Docket 82; p. 164 (#M42654); 15 Jul. 1970)] [RP037]

[97]Certificate of Marriage of William Charles Rucker and Vendela Xvelyn Olson, NJ State Bureau of Vital Statistics. [RP037]

[98]Letter from R. J. Dohm; 19 Jul. 1995, *op. cit.*; Soc. Sec. Death Records,

op. cit. In the Dohm letter, Vendela's date of death is reported as "DIED 3/5/85;" in the Social Security record it is reported as "03-00-1984." In a second letter postmarked 04 Oct. 1997, R. J. Dohm stated, "Sorry about the mistake. Vendela died 3-5-84."

[99]Death Certificate of Vendela Rucker, New Jersey State Dept. of Health No. 11934. [RP037]

[100]Obituary, *The Record*, p. A-10 (06 Mar. 1984). [RP037]

[101]Certificate of Death of Charles Rucker, Florida State File No. 80-070474; Local File No. 00137. [RP033] The date of birth for Charles Rucker (Jr.) is given on his death certificate as "July 31, 1907." This is consistent with the date of birth given in his Social Security file [Soc. Sec. Death Records, *op. cit.*], but it does not agree with his baptismal record, in which his birth is reported as 31 July 190**8**. Since the latter record is closer to the time of the event, it is presumed to be the correct one. Moreover, Frances (née Rucker) Skelton, who was born 04 April 1908, recalls her cousin, Charles, attending the same classes as she throughout grammar school.

[102]Taped interview with Mary Frotscher and Frances Skelton on 10 May 1997, *op. cit.*

[103]SDA Pilzeň Register of the Parish, Book No. 28, Horažd'ovice Parish; p. 17.

[104]World War I draft registration card of Adolf Rücker, *op cit.*

[105]Records of the Maple Grove Park Cemetery, *op. cit.*

[106]Certificate of Marriage Registration between Adolf Rücker and Matylda Prihodova, New York, City of New York, Borough of Manhattan; Marriage Register No. HD-13340-04-rk. [RP005]

[107]Czech Marriage Certificate of Adolf Rücker and Matylda Prihoda, *op cit.*

[108]SDA Třeboň Register of the Parish, Book No. 9, Velká Chýška Parish; p. 348.

[109]Records of the Maple Grove Park Cemetery, *op. cit.*

[110]New York Passenger List, April 27 - 29, 1903, Vol. 601-602, List K, p. 159, line 19; National Archives Microfilm Publication T715, Roll 348.

[111]Declaration of Intention No. 595, filed 31 Mar. 1910 at the Bergen County, NJ Court House in Hackensack, NJ.

[112]Bergen Co., NJ, Immigration and Naturalization Records, Vol. 7, No. 1669, issued 23 June 1916.

[113]World War I draft registration card of Adolf Rücker, *op cit.*

[114]1910 U.S. Census (population), New Jersey, Bergen Co., Lodi Twp., Little Ferry Borough, Super. Dist. 178; Enum. Dist. 31, p. 22A, dwell. 364; visit. 409; National Archives Microfilm Publication T624, Roll 869.

1920 U.S. Census (population), New Jersey, Bergen Co., Little Ferry Borough, Super. Dist. 6; Enum. Dist. 38, p. 21B, dwell. 333; visit. 444; National Archives Microfilm Publication T625, Roll 1018.

[115]Baptismal Record Book, Church of the Immaculate Conception, 49 Vreeland Ave., Hackensack, NJ, p. 54, No. 1166.

[116]Death Certificate of Caroline Komarek, No. 31034, NJ State Bureau of Vital Statistics. [RP030]

[117]Letter from R. J. Dohm; 19 Jul. 1995, *op. cit.*

[118]Marriage Record Book, Church of the Immaculate Conception, p. 28, No. 706.

[119]Death Certificate of Rudolf Komarek; Commonwealth of Kentucky, Certificate of Death File No. 116 87 06156; Registrar's No. 1159; Registration Dist. No. 755; Primary Registration Dist. No. 2275. The date of burial specified on the death certificate is "Feb 23, 1998". This conflicts with the date of death, "Feb 20, 1987", the date

signed by the certifying physician, "3/2/87"; and the date of registration, "Mar 5 1987." The year of burial, 1998, is obviously in error.

[120]Baptismal Record Book, Church of the Immaculate Conception, p. 69, No. 1514.

[121]Newport, Campbell County, KY; Marriage Book 131, p. 406. [RP031]

[122]A record for the birth of William Franklin Frotscher has not been located. On 24 June 1997, the Kentucky Historical Society Library reported the following in a letter to the author: "We searched our vital statistics files and our 1910 census records and found nothing on William Frotscher." [RP031] Nevertheless, William is recorded living at 925 Third St., Dayton, KY, with his parents, 3 living brothers, and 4 living sisters in the 1910 census; the census citation follows.

[123]1910 U.S. Census (population), Kentucky, Campbell Co., Dayton City, Enum. Dist. 43, p. 152, 925 Third St.; visit. 41; fam. 48; National Archives Microfilm Publication T624, Roll 467.

[124]Certificate of Death of William F. Frotscher, Sr., PA State File No. 003610; filed 28 Jan. 1990. [RP031]

[125]New Jersey Bureau of Vital Statistics, Certificate and Record of birth, No. 191, dated 12 February 1909.

[126]Baptismal Record Book, Church of the Immaculate Conception, p. 69, No. 1515.

[127]Certificate of Marriage from the Evangelical Congregational Church, corner of Main St. and Marshall Ave., Little Ferry, NJ; certificate is signed by Rev. F. V. MacPeck and witnessed by Caroline Komarek and Edward Rucker.

[128]Commonwealth of Kentucky, Certificate of Birth No. 11768; filed 24 Sep. 1940.

[129]Death Certificate of Floyd Skelton; Commonwealth of Pennsylvania, State File No. 090118

[130]Honorable Discharge Certificate, U.S. Army, issued 19 Oct. 1945 at the Separation Center, Fort Dix, NJ; No. 32,762,959.

[131]Taped interview on 05 November 1995 with Adolph Rucker and Frances (née Rucker) Skelton at the Rucker family home at 135 Washington Avenue, Little Ferry, NJ.

[132]Records of the New York Cemetery, Hackensack, NJ; Plot Nos. 35 and 35N, Sect. E, Grave 23.

[133]Letter from David Kohout; 13 May 1998, *op. cit.*

[134]*Ibid.* As of May 1998, the address for Marie (née Nová) Rückerová, widow of Václav Rücker, is Nábřežni 270, 341 01 Horažďovice, Czech Republic; telephone: (Czech Republic) + 0187 + 51 34 21.

[135]*Ibid.* As of May 1998, the address for Mr. Jaroslav Rücker is Nádřažni 308, 340 21 Janovice nad Úhlavou, Czech Republic; telephone: (Czech Republic) + 0186 + 69 22 78.

[136]*New York Cemetery, Hackensack, Bergen County, New Jersey* (New York, NY: Casper C. Childs, Printer, 178 Fulton St., 1851), 1.

[137]Bergen County Deed Book 815, p. 589.

[138]As previously noted, sometime between 1916 and 1918 the forename of Adolf Rucker was unofficially changed from "Adolf" to "Otto."

[139]Citations to the sources for genealogical records are given in the section "Genealogical Summary: Family of Jan Příhoda and Žofie Zimová"

[140]As previously noted, all Czech records reported in this genealogy were uncovered by Mr. David Kohout.

[141]SDA Třeboň Register of the Parish, Book No. 2, Soběslav Parish; p. 126.

[142]SDA Třeboň Register of the Parish, Book No. 3, Soběslav Parish; p. 9.

[143]SDA Třeboň Register of the Parish, Book No. 3, Soběslav Parish; p. 293. Only the period 1757-1761 was searched for siblings of Martin and Mathias.

[144]SDA Třeboň Register of the Parish, Book No. 5, Soběslav Parish; p. 23.

[145]Serfdomers were not slaves, but they were bound to the land and to the lord of the manor to which they were attached. Their lord could neither evict them from the manor, nor sell them, as long as they performed their half of the bargain, tilling the land and rendering other services to the manor. On the other hand, the serf were bound to the soil, *i.e.*, they could not leave the manor, even if dissatisfied with conditions or forced to live under the rule of a cruel and lawless lord. Joseph Ward Swain, *The Harper History of Civilization. op. cit.,* Vol. I, p. 425.

[146]SDA Třeboň Register of the Parish, Book No. 1, Nedvědice Parish; p. 24.

[147]SDA Třeboň Register of the Parish, Book No. 1, Nedvědice Parish; p. 66.

[148]SDA Třeboň Register of the Parish, Book No. 3, Soběslav Parish; p. 374.

[149]SDA Třeboň Register of the Parish, Book No. 1, Nedvědice Parish; p. 24.

[150]SDA Třeboň Register of the Parish, Book No. 11, Velká Chýška Parish; p. 49.

[151]SDA Třeboň Register of the Parish, Book No. 11, Velká Chýška Parish; p. 49.

[152]SDA Třeboň Register of the Parish, Book No. 8, Velká Chýška Parish; p. 20.

[153]SDA Třeboň Register of the Parish, Book No. 9, Velká Chýška Parish; p. 348.

[154]Family Bible record, originated by Matylda (née Příhodova) Rücker, now

maintained by her daughter, Mary (née Rucker) Frotscher at her home in Newburg, PA.

[155]SDA Třeboň Christening Register, Velká Chýška Parish

[156]Electronic-mail message from Josef C. Masek to the author dated 21 Aug. 1997 - 23:02:50 EDT; hereinafter referred to as "Electronic mail from J. C. Masek; 21 Aug. 1997." [RP036]

[157]1900 U.S. Census (population), Illinois, Cook Co., West Town (Ward 8), Super. Dist. 1; Enum. Dist. 211, p. 19, dwell. 113; fam. 400; National Archives Microfilm Publication T623, Roll 253.

[158]The surname is spelt "Balwin" on death certificate of Bedrick Prihoda, but as "Balvin" on death certificate of Marie (née Balvin) Prihoda and as "Balvin" on birth certificate of Jerome Prihoda.

[159]1900 U.S. Census (population), Illinois, Cook Co., West Town (Ward 8), Super. Dist. 1; Enum. Dist. 211, p. 19, dwell. 113; fam. 400; National Archives Microfilm Publication T623, Roll 253.

[160]1920 U.S. Census (population), Illinois, Cook Co., Chicago (48th Pct.), Enum. Dist. 2157, Sheet 5, Line 57; dwell. 59; fam. 102; National Archives Microfilm Publication T625, Roll 354.

[161]Soc. Sec. Death Records, *op. cit.*

[162]Death Certificate of Mary M. Prihoda, Indiana State Board of Health, Local No. MC 125; No. 89-9713; filed 20 Mar. 1989. [RP034]

[163]Letter from Frances Law Smith of Michigan City, IN, a step daughter of Jerome Prihoda, dated 28 August 1997, to the author; hereinafter cited as "Letter from Frances Law Smith; 28 Aug. 1997." [RP034]

[164]Death Certificate of Mary M. Prihoda, *op. cit.* and Soc. Sec. Death Records, *op. cit.*

[165]Statement of Service for Jerome Prihoda, Service No. 2351201, supplied to the author on 17 Sep. 1997 by the National Archives and Records Administration, National Personnel

Records Center (Military Personnel Records), 9700 Page Ave., St. Louis, MO 63132-5100. [RP034]

[166]Letter from Frances Law Smith; 28 Aug. 1997, *op. cit.*

[167]Death Certificate of Leona B. Prihoda, Indiana State Board of Health, Local No. MC 092; No. 76-005365; filed 27 Feb. 1976. [RP034]

[168]Czech Marriage Certificate of Adolf Rücker and Matylda Prihoda, *op. cit.*

[169]On the reverse side of the photograph, the following is printed: "From the Studio Henry D. Schoerry 43, Ave. A. Cor. 3rd St. New York. Duplicates can be had at any time."

[170]Bergen Co., NJ Deed Book 64, p. 561.

[171]Bergen Co., NJ Bond Book (28 Sep. 1906)

[172]Bergen Co., NJ Deed Book 64, p. 561.

[173]In this work, *Adolf Rucker* refers to the father, *Adolph Rucker* refers to the son.

[174]Maple Grove Park Cemetery records, *op. cit.*

[175]*Immaculate Conception Church 100th Anniversary 1891 - 1991* (Cleveland, TN: The National Directory Services for Catholic Parishes, 1991), p. 3.

[176]Baptismal Register, Church of the Immaculate Conception, Vol. I, p. 69, No. 1515.

[177]Letter from Rev. Thomas F. Lynch, Pastor of the Immaculate Conception Church, dated 13 June 1996 to the author. Rev. Lynch stated: "I regret to say, we have no record of a Baptism for Edward Rucker."

[178]Mary (née Rucker) Frotscher has a clear recollection that the wedding took place at St. Margaret's Church on Washington Ave., in Little Ferry. Records of the marriage however are in the Church of the Immaculate Conception on Vreeland Avenue in Hackensack, NJ.

[179]Declaration of Intention No. 9524(?), filed 16 January 1922 at the Bergen County, NJ Court House in Hackensack, NJ.

[180]Some information about Rudolph Komarek has been taken, with permission, from a book being written by William F. Frotscher, Jr. regarding the exploits of Rudolph Arthur Komarek, the elder son of Rudolph and Carolina (née Rucker) Komarek. Other information was obtained from Robert Edwin Komarek, the younger son of Rudolph and Carrie, during a telephone conversation with the author on 15 July 1996.

[181]Certificate of Naturalization of Rudolph Komarek, No. 2236515, Certificate No. 196092, issued by the Common Pleas Court of Bergen County for the State of New Jersey at Hackensack, NJ on 29 January 1926.

[182]Sporting License for Soaring No. 1203, issued by The Soaring Society of America, Inc., Federation Aeronautique Internationale.

[183]The property was located at 830 Beachview Dr., Jekyll Island, Glynn Co., GA.

[184]Death Certificate of Rudolph Komarek, *op cit.*

[185]Letter from Mary Frotscher; 17 Jun. 1996., *op. cit.*

[186]William Franklin Frotscher, Sr. *Dad's Stories Tales of Growing up on the banks of the Ohio and other stories* (Newburg, PA: Privately printed, 1998), 196 pp. [Chapter 16 is reproduced here with permission of William Franklin Frotscher, Jr.]

[187]Bergen Co., NJ Mortgage Book 1797, p. 213, 11 Feb. 1941.

[188]"Bohemian Actors Stage A Success," *Bergen Evening Record*, p. 13 (17 Jan. 1927). [RP010]

[189]At the time, the Atlantic and Pacific Tea Company maintained a chain of retail grocery stores known as "A & P."

[190]William Franklin Frotscher, Sr. *Dad's Stories, op cit.* [Chapter 18 is reproduced here with permission of William Franklin Frotscher, Jr.]

[191]*Masters, Mates, Pilots, and Engineers of Merchant Steam Vessels,* (Washington, DC: US Government Printing Office, 1895), 179. Masters License No. A47055, issued 28 Oct. 1895.

[192]Bergen Co., NJ Mortgage Book 2228, p. 247, 14 Oct. 1947.

[193]Adolph chose to spell his forename with a "ph" at the end rather than an "f." When asked why, he said to make it different from Hitler.

[194]Certification of Military Service of Edward E. Rucker issued 30 Oct. 1997 by the National Personnel Records Center, National Archives and Records Administration, St. Louis, MO 63132-5100. [RP019]

[195]Details of the activities of the 473rd Anti-Aircraft Artillery Battalion during World War II are taken from the book *473rd AAA On Target — Battle Participation 1944 — 1945* (Munich, Germany: R. Oldenbourg, 1945). The book was written by the officers and men of the Battalion. [RP019]

[196]Enlisted Record and Report of Separation - Honorable Discharge of Edward E. Rucker, Army Serial No. 32 762 959 (dated 19 Oct. 1945). [RP019]

[197]*Ibid.,* 11.

[198]*Ibid.,* 17.

[199]Certification of Military Service of E. E. Rucker, *op. cit.*

[200]In the will of Matylda (née Prihodova) Rucker which she signed on 08 Nov. 1946, she refers to her sons as "Adolph Rucker and Edward Rucker," Adolph being spelt with "ph." [Bergen Co. Book 187, 451.]

[201]Information regarding the actions of the 459th Fighter Squadron was taken from the book *Combat Digest 33rd Fighter Group.* [No author, publisher, or date of publication given. Based on the content, the book probably was published in the latter part of 1945.]

[202]The source of some information about the early life of Joseph C. Masek is Mary (née Rucker) Frotscher during a telephone conversation with the author on 31 May 1997. See also: Electronic mail from J. C. Masek; 21 Aug. 1997, *op. cit.*

[203]*la Mère Michelle,* 14482 Big Ben Basin, Saratoga, CA 95070.

[204]Joseph Izzo, Jr. "A Perfect 4-Star Feast in Saratoga," in the Arts and Books Section of the *San Jose Mercury News,* 04 Mar. 1997.

[205]Taken from an article entitled "The Resurrection of Rudy," by John L. Behler, Curator, Department of Herpetology, Bronx Zoo, Bronx, New York City, NY. The complete article was published in *Notes from Noah,* Vol. XI, No. 4 (1984), pp. 23-26.

[206]Taken, with permission, from work in progress by William F. Frotscher, Jr. in which the life and exploits of Rudolph Arthur Komarek are chronicled and discussed.

[207]Letter from Lt. Gen. Frank F. Ledford, Jr., M.D., Medical Corps, dated 10 Apr. 1991, to Mr. Rudy Komarek, P.O. Box 334, Ridgefield Park, NJ 07660.

[208]W. S. Brown, L. Jones, and R. Stechert, *Bull. Chicago Herp. Soc.* **29,** No. 4, 74-79 (1994).

[209]Rudy Komarek, *Bull. Chicago Herp. Soc.* **29,** No. 4, 211-212 (1994).

[210]W. S. Brown, L. Jones, and R. Stechert, *Bull. Chicago Herp. Soc.* **29,** No. 4, 212-214 (1994).

[211]Gautam Naik, "Herpetologists Think Poacher of Rattler Is Lower Than a Snake," in *The Wall Street Journal,* pp. A1 & A8 (15 Nov. 1995).

[212]Peggy Thompson, "Rudy the Rattler Wrangler," in *The News-Chronicle,* Shippensburg, PA 17257, 03 July 1995, p. 1.

[213]Mac Cordell, "State Sinks Fangs into Snake Man," in *The News-Chronicle*, Shippensburg, PA 17257, 22 Aug. 1996, pp. 1 & 3.

[214]The acronym POSSLQ, pronounced *"pos-l-que,"* was coined by the U.S. Census Bureau. It stands for "Persons of Opposite Sex Sharing Living Quarters." For further details, see Judith Martin, *Miss Manners' Guide to Excruciatingly Correct Behavior.* (New York, NY: Atheneum, 1982), 299.

[215]William F. Frotscher, Jr. *Growing Up Together. Life in Maywood, N.J. during the 1940's as Seen by a Young Boy* (Newburg, PA: Privately printed, 1993), 30 pp.

[216] E. F. Skelton, "High Pressure Science and Technology in Japan," *Scientific Monograph*, ed. B. J. McDonald, pub. by the Department of the Navy, Office of Naval Research - Tokyo (ONRT-M1), July 1978 (130 pages).

[217]E. F. Skelton and A. W. Webb, "High Pressure Research," in *Encyclopedia of Physical Science and Technology*, Vol. 11, pp. 256-276 (1986).

[218]N. E. Moulton and E. F. Skelton, "Effects of Pressure on Thallium-Based Superconductors," Chapter 21 in *Thallium-Based High Temperature Superconductors*, eds. A. K. Hermann and J. V. Yakhmi (New York, NY: Marcel Dekker, Inc., 1993), pp. 433-450.

[219][1] "Method of Making Tl-Sr-Ca-Cu-Oxide Superconductors Comprising Heating at Elevated Pressures in a Sealed Container," Patent No. 5,120,704 (awarded 09 June 1992); [2] "Stabilized Zirconia - CoCrAlY Coating," Patent No. 5,147,731 (awarded 15 Sep. 1992); [3] "High T_c Copper-Oxide Superconductors Comprising Tl-Sr-Ca-Cu-O," Patent No. 5,298,484 (awarded 29 Mar. 1994); [4] "High Temperature Mercury-Containing Superconductors and Method of Making Same," Patent No. 5,776,861 (awarded 07 July 1998); and [5] "Zinc Oxide Stabilized Zirconia," Patent No. 5,800,934 (awarded 01 Sep. 1998).

[220]Hon. Ike Skelton, "Physicist, Dr. Earl F. Skelton, Honored," *Congressional Record* [U.S. House of Representatives], 16 June 1995, p. E1274.

[221]Earl F. Skelton, "The John Skelton — Catharine Hepler Family: From the Shenandoah to the Midwest," *National Genealogical Society Quarterly* 80 (December 1992): 245-264.

[222]Isaac Newton Skelton-III and Earl Franklin Skelton, *Ike, This Is You, A History of the Skelton, Boone, Barry, Beach, Blattner, Corum, Hoagland, Lehew, Strode, Wright, and Young Families* (Washington, DC: Privately published, 1995), (223 pages).

[223]Certification No. 400 issued 01 Apr. 1997 by the Board for Certification of Genealogists, P. O. Box 14921, Washington, DC 20044.

[224]William R. Steng, "All Ham!", *Bergen Evening Record*, 31 Aug. 1957, p. 2.

[225]*Ibid.*

[226]Alan M. Schlein and Audrey Wennblom, "Marine Precision Carries the Day: Marathon Goes Off Without a Hitch," in *The Washington Post*, 02 Nov. 1981, p. C2.

[227]Bill Kamenjar, "Marine Corps Marathon: On Hitting the Wall," in *The Fairfax Journal*, 03 Nov. 1981, p. A13; John Henkel, "NRL 'Marathon Man' Breaks Record," in *Labstracts*, Vol. XXI, No. 45, p. 1 (06 Nov. 1981). (*Labstracts* is an official publication of the Naval Research Laboratory in Washington, DC.)

[228]Michael Hill, "The Second Largest Marathon in America," in *Runner's World*, Vol. 17, No. 2 (Feb. 1982), p. 30; Jim Elliott, "Marine Marathon," in *Track Master*, Vol. 4, No. 11 (Dec. 1981), p. 13.

[229]QST (Official Journal of the American Radio Relay League, Newington, CT), Nov. 1981, p. 87; Auto-Call (Official Journal of the Foundation for Amateur Radio, Arlington, VA), Oct. 1981, p. 28.
[230]The feat was accomplished twice: On 04 Nov. 1979, the marathon was run in 3 hr., 42 min., 32 sec. (3:42:32) and 55 radio contacts were completed; on 01 Nov. 1981, the marathon was run in 3:37:41 and 70 communications were completed — including some with hams in Europe and the U.S.S.R. [Ref.: Letters to Mr. Colin Smith, Editor; Guinness Book of Records, 2 Cecil Ct., London Rd., Enfield, Middlesex EN2 6DJ, England, dated 02 Jan. 1980 and 17 May 1982, from the author; and Mr. Smith's replies of 23 Jan. 1980 and 28 May 1982.] Sandwiched between these two events, Earl ran his fastest marathon — the date was 02 Nov. 1980 and the time was 3:02:11. [In the year 2000, Earl will become a sexagenarian; he also will complete his 50th marathon and his 20th Marine Corps Marathon.]
[231]Earl F. Skelton, Carol's Legacy (Washington, DC: Privately published, 1996), 31 pp. The epilogue in Carol's Legacy describes how, thirty years after Carol's death, Earl searched for and found Carol's mother, then living in Georga. Through an exchange of correspondence a catharsis was reached.
[232]On 04 Sep. 1988 in Washington, DC, Phylisa Rudich married Curtis Mark Bolak. Today they have two daughters, both of whom were born in Atlanta, GA: Doralyn Rose on 29 Sep. 1993 and Jillian Meraina on 14 Aug. 1995.
[233]Program, 1997 International Health Congress, sponsored by the World Health Organization and the State of Maryland, Baltimore, MD, 15-17 Sep. 1997, pp. 11 & 22.
[234]The Lancet (245 West 17th Street, New York, NY 10011), Vol. 350, p. 942 (27 Sep. 1997).

[235]High School Equivalency Diploma No. G012462, issued May 1998 by the Education Department of The University of the State of New York, Albany, NY.
[236]At the time of her birth, the Ukraine was part of the Union of Soviet Socialist Republics.
[237]Certificate of Naturalization of Dana Segal Skelton, No. 22501671 (INS Reg. No. A70 326 826).
[238][Shippensburg, PA] News Chronicle - 02 Aug. 1995.
[239]All Czech records reported in this genealogy were found by David Kohout, a professional genealogist, op cit.
[240]SDA Třeboň Register of the Parish, Book No. 1, Soběslav Parish; p. 79. Alphabetic register of records of the parish of Soběslav, Register No. 49. "I did not search this record, but [it] is possible that in this record will be mentioned the fathers of Jan Příhoda and Žofie Zimová. The parish records of the parish Soběslav begin in the year 1639, however there is no mention any marriage of anyone from the Příhoda family for the period 1639-1690." D. Kohout, 21 Aug. 1997.
[241]Ibid., Book No. 2, Soběslav Parish; p. 126.
[242]Ibid.
[243]Ibid., Book No. 3, Soběslav Parish; p. 9.
[244]Ibid.,, Book No. 3, Soběslav Parish; p. 293. Only the period 1757-1761 was searched for siblings of Martin and Mathias.
[245]Ibid.
[246]Ibid.,, Book No. 1, Nedvědice Parish; p. 66.
[247]SDA Třeboň Register of the Parish, Book No. 5, Soběslav Parish; p. 23.
[248]Ibid.,, Book No. 3, Soběslav Parish; p. 374.
[249]Ibid.,, Book No. 1, Nedvědice Parish; p. 49.
[250]Ibid.,, Book No. 1, Nedvědice Parish; p. 24.

251*Ibid.*
252*Ibid.,*, Book No. 13, Soběslav Parish; p. 32.
253*Ibid.*
254*Ibid.,*, Book No. 1, Nedvědice Parish; p. 68.
255*Ibid.,*, Book No. 2, Nedvědice Parish; p. 51.
256*Ibid.*
257SDA Třeboň Register of the Parish, Book No. 11, Velká Chýška Parish; p. 49.
258*Ibid.,*, Book No. 8, Velká Chýška Parish; p. 20.
259Prihoda family Bible record. Bible is presently in the possession of Mary (née Rucker) Frotscher of Newburg, PA.
260SDA Třeboň Register of the Parish, Book No. 9, Velká Chýška Parish; p. 348.
261*Ibid.*
262Report of David Kohout dated 04 Sep. 1997, p. 1.
263Family Bible record, originated by Matylda (née Přihodova) Rücker, now maintained by her daughter, Mary (née Rucker) Frotscher at her home in Newburg, PA.
264SDA Třeboň Christening Register, Velká Chýška Parish
265SDA Třeboň Register of the Parish, Book No. 9, Velká Chýška Parish; p. 348.
266Letter from Joseph Masek of Saratoga, CA, dated 12 Nov. 1994, to the author: "My grandfather Jan Prihoda died November 22nd 1939, having suffered of asthma."
267See letter from Mrs. Vilma (née Prihoda) Maier of Prague dated 12 June 1947 to Mrs. Leona (née Barnett) (Law) Prihoda of Michigan City, Indiana. [A translation of this letter is given on pp. 59-60 of this work.]
268In a letter written in 1945 by Mrs. Mary (née Rucker) Frotscher to her brother, Edward Rucker, then serving with the U.S. Army in Europe, the following statements are made: "These are addresses of Mom's relatives in Prague. One is Mom's niece - your cousin [Vilemina Mayróva]. Other is your cousin - (a son of another niece) [Joseph Mãsek]. They both are daughters of Mom's brother John Prihoda who has since died. Vilemina Mayróva, Praha II Podskalsak 57 and Joseph Mãsek, Praha III Tomassha $27^1/_2$ ..."
269Electronic mail from J. C. Masek; 21 Aug. 1997, *op. cit.*; see also the letter from Mrs. Maier dated 12 June 1947, *op. cit.*
270Indiana State Board of Health; Certificate of Death filed 02 January 1948; Reg. No. 1550. The information given in 1948 in the death certificate for her son, Bedrick Prihoda, specifies that Bedrick's mother's name was "Jana Balwin." The informant was Jerome Prihoda, a son of Bedrick. However, "Balwin" is also the maiden surname given for Bedrick's wife, née Mary Balwin. This is confirmed in other records. The name of Balwin for the maiden name of Bedrick's mother (also Karel's second wife), is believed to be an error.
271Bederick Prihoda Certificate of Death, Indiana State Board of Health; filed 02 January 1948; Reg. No. 1550. [RP034]
272Marriage Certificate of Bedřich Prihoda and Mary Balvin, No. 127334, Marriage Records, Cook Co., IL. [RP034]
273Indiana State Board of Health; Certificate of Death filed 12 April 1934; Reg. No. 12095. [RP034]
274Certificate of Birth for Jaroslav Prihoda on 16 July 1895, State of Illinois, No. 116837; filed 13 February 1942. [RP034]
2751900 U.S. Census (population), Illinois, Cook Co., West Town - Ward 8, Super. Dist. 1; Enum. Dist. 211, p. 19, dwell. 113; fam. 400; National Archives Microfilm Publication T623, Roll 253.

Since Bedrick and Marie were married in 1888 in Chicago and since their oldest child, Jennie, was reported as born in Nov. 1889 in Illinois, it is likely that Bedrick came to America before 1890.

[276]No Soundex index exists for Indiana for the 1910 census. The microfilm record for Michigan City, La Porte County, Indiana [National Archives Microfilm Publication T624, Roll 363] has been searched by the author thrice. No family named Prihoda has been found, however several pages of this microfilm record are illegible.

[277]1920 U.S. Census (population), Indiana, La Porte Co., Michigan City, Super. Dist. 13; Enum. Dist. 144, p. 2B, dwell. 220; visit. 36; fam. 38; National Archives Microfilm Publication T625, Roll 447.

[278]Jaroslav Prihoda Birth Certificate; Cook Co., IL, Reg. Dist. No. 3104; Certif. No. 116837; filed 13 Feb. 1942. Three certificates, each dated 17 June 1997, have been issued by the Cook County Clerk stating that a three year search for a birth record in Chicago and Cook County, Illinois has been made with negative results for Jennie (1889-1891); Charles (1891-1893); and Peter (1897-1899). (The certificate for Jaroslav was created in 1942, during World War II, probably to comply a security requirement.) [RP034]

[279]Birth dates of the four children of Bedrick and Marie are from a family Bible in the possession of Mary (née Rucker) Frotscher of Newburg, PA.

[280]Letter from Frances Law Smith; 28 Aug. 1997, *op. cit.*

[281]SDA Třeboň Register of the Parish, Book No. 9, Velká Chýška Parish; p. 348.

[282]Records of the Maple Grove Park Cemetery (formerly The New York Cemetery), 535 Hudson St., Hackensack, NJ; Plot Nos. 35 and 35N, Sect. E.

[283]Certificate of Marriage Registration between Adolf Rücker and

Matylda Prihodova, New York, City of New York, Borough of Manhattan; Marriage Register No. HD-13340-04-rk. [RP005]

[284]SDA Pilzeň Register of the Parish, Book No. 28, Horažd'ovic Parish; p. 17.

[285]World War I draft registration card of Adolf Rücker, *op. cit.*

[286]Records of the Maple Grove Park Cemetery (formerly The New York Cemetery), 535 Hudson St., Hackensack, NJ; Lot Nos. 35 and 35N, Sect. E.

[287]1910 U.S. Census (population), New Jersey, Bergen Co., Lodi Twp., Little Ferry Borough, Super. Dist. 178; Enum. Dist. 31, p. 22A, dwell. 364; visit. 409; National Archives Microfilm Publication T624, Roll 869.

1920 U.S. Census (population), New Jersey, Bergen Co., Little Ferry Borough, Super. Dist. 6; Enum. Dist. 38, p. 21B, dwell. 333; visit. 444; National Archives Microfilm Publication T625, Roll 1018.

[288]Certificate and Record of Birth of Edward Rucker, New Jersey State Bureau of Vital Statistics; filed 01 Aug. 1909; dated 02 July 1927.

[289]Honorable Discharge Certificate, U.S. Army, issued 19 Oct. 1945 at the Separation Center, Fort Dix, NJ; No. 32,762,959.

[290]The date of birth is based upon family records. No record exists in the New Jersey Department of Health and Senior Services for a birth of Adolf Rucker during the year 1910.

[291]Records of the Maple Grove Park Cemetery (formerly The New York Cemetery), 535 Hudson St., Hackensack, NJ; Plot Nos. 35 and 35N, Sect. E, Grave 23.

[292]All information about the Mašek family has been taken from a family history chart starting with Martin Mašek (1715-1780). A copy of this chart was kindly provided via FAX transmission to the author on 13 Aug. 1997 by Joseph

Mašek of Saratoga, CA, a great-great-great-grandson of Martin Mašek.

²⁹³Marriage Certificate of George Kripner and Jennie Prihoda, No. 626298, Cook Co., IL. [RP039]

²⁹⁴1920 U.S. Census (population), Illinois, Cook Co., Chicago (48th Pct.), Enum. Dist. 2157, Sheet 5, Line 57; dwell. 59; fam. 102; National Archives Microfilm Publication T625, Roll 354.

²⁹⁵Interview with Mary (née Rucker) Frotscher and Frances (née Rucker) Skelton in Newburg, PA on Saturday, 10 May 1997. The interview was tape recorded.

²⁹⁶Soc. Sec. Death Records, *op. cit.*

²⁹⁷Death Certificate of Gerald Kripner, No. 83 058692; Division of Vital Records, Illinois Dept. of Public Health. [RP039]

²⁹⁸Soc. Sec. Death Records, *op. cit.*

²⁹⁹Death Certificate of Charles Prihoda, No. 73-010126; Indiana State Board of Health. [RP034]

³⁰⁰Death Certificate of Mary M. Prihoda, No. 89-009713; Indiana State Board of Health. [RP034]

³⁰¹Letter from Frances Law Smith; 28 Aug. 1997, *op. cit.*

³⁰²Interview with Mary Frotscher and Frances Skelton; 10 May 1997, *op. cit.*

³⁰³Death Certificate of Jerome Prihoda, No. 71-021786; Indiana State Board of Health. [RP034]

³⁰⁴Soc. Sec. Death Records, *op. cit.*

³⁰⁵Death Certificate of Leona B. Prihoda, No. 76-005365; Indiana State Board of Health. [RP034]

³⁰⁶Letter from Frances Law Smith; 28 Aug. 1997, *op. cit.*

³⁰⁷Statement of Service for Jerome Prihoda, Service No. 2351201, supplied to the author on 17 Sep. 1997 by the National Archives and Records Administration, National Personnel Records Center (Military Personnel Records), 9700 Page Ave., St. Louis, MO 63132-5100. [RP034]

³⁰⁸Interview with Mary Frotscher and Frances Skelton; 10 May 1997, *op. cit.*

³⁰⁹Baptismal Record Book, Church of the Immaculate Conception, 49 Vreeland Ave., Hackensack, NJ, p. 54, No. 1166.

³¹⁰Death Certificate of Caroline Komarek, No. 31034, NJ State Bureau of Vital Statistics. [RP030]

³¹¹Letter from R. J. Dohm; 19 Jul. 1995, *op. cit.*

³¹²Mary (née Rucker) Frotscher has a clear recollection that the wedding took place at St. Margaret's Church on Washington Ave., in Little Ferry. Records of the marriage however are in the Church of the Immaculate Conception on Vreeland Avenue in Hackensack, NJ.

³¹³Marriage Record Book, Church of the Immaculate Conception, p. 28, No. 706.

³¹⁴Declaration of Intention No. 9524(?), filed 16 January 1922 at the Bergen County, NJ Court House in Hackensack, NJ. Copies of the naturalizaiton papers (Declaration of Intention, Petition for Naturalization, and Certificate of Naturalization) were received under the Freedon of Information Act from the U.S. Department of Justice. [RP030]

³¹⁵Marriage Licence of Rudolph Komarek and Carolina Rucker, No. 173, NJ State Bureau of Vital Statistics. [RP030]

³¹⁶Death Certificate of Rudolph Komarek; File No. 116 87 06156, Registrar's No. 1159, Dept. of Health Services, Commonwealth of Kentucky. [RP030]

³¹⁷Birth Certificate of Rudolph Arthur Komarek; No. 367, Reg. No. 736; State Dept. of Health, Bureau of Vital Statistics, NJ. On this birth certificate, the name of the father is given as "Ralph Komarek," not Rudolph Komarek. The forename "Ralph" is believed to be a typographical error. [RP007}

[318]Baptismal Record Book, Church of the Immaculate Conception, p. 69, No. 1514.

[319]Newport, Campbell County, KY; Marriage Book 131, p. 406. [RP031]

[320]A record for William Franklin Frotscher's birth has not been located. On 24 June 1997, the Kentucky Historical Society Library reported the following in a letter to the author: "We searched our vital statistics files and our 1910 census records and found nothing on William Frotscher." [RP031] Nevertheless, William is recorded living at 925 Third St., Dayton, KY, with his parents, 3 living brothers, and 4 living sisters in the 1910 census. A citation to this census reference follows.

[321]1910 U.S. Census (population), Kentucky, Campbell Co., Dayton City, Enum. Dist. 43, p. 152, 925 Third St.; visit. 41; fam. 48; National Archives Microfilm Publication T624, Roll 467.

[322]Certificate of Death of William F. Frotscher, Sr., Pennsylvania State File No. 003610; filed 28 Jan. 1990. [RP031]

[323]Birth Certificate of Frances Rucker; New Jersey Bureau of Vital Statistics, Certificate and Record of birth, No. 191, dated 12 February 1909. [RP010]

[324]Baptismal Record Book, Church of the Immaculate Conception, p. 69, No. 1515.

[325]Certificate of Marriage from the Evangelical Congregational Church, corner of Main St. and Marshall Ave., Little Ferry, NJ; certificate is signed by Rev. F. V. MacPeck and witnessed by Caroline Komarek and Edward Rucker. [RP010]

[326]Birth Certificate of Floyd Skelton; Commonwealth of Kentucky, Certificate of Birth No. 14768; filed 24 Sep. 1940. [RP032]

[327]Marriage Certificate of Floyd Skelton and Frances Rucker, No. 481, Bueaau of Vital Statistics, NJ. [RP032]

[328]Death Certificate of Floyd Skelton; Commonwealth of Pennsylvania, State File No. 090118

[329]Electronic mail from J. C. Masek; 21 Aug. 1997, *op. cit.*

[330]*Ibid.*

[331]Birth Certificate of Barbara Marie Anna Masek, Dept. of Health Services, CA; File No. 62-353837; Reg. & Certif. Nos. 3801 & 18423. [RP036]

[332]Birth Certificate of Joseph Marc Andre Masek, Dept. of Health Services, CA; File No. 65-258805; Reg. & Certif. Nos. 3801 & 13207. [RP036]

[333]Mašek family history kindly provided by FAX transmission on 13 Aug. 1997 by Joseph Mašek of Saratoga, CA, *op. cit.*

[334]Birth Certificate of Robert Edwin Komarek, State Dept. of Health, Bureau of Vital Statistics, NJ. On this birth certificate, the mother is listed as "Caroline Ann Rucker." This is the first, and only, time the middle name of "Ann" is seen in the official records. [RP018]

[335]Marriage Certificate of Robert Komarek and Sally Ann French, No. 26113, NJ State Dept. of Health. [RP018]

[336]Birth Certificate of Sally Ann French, State Dept. of Health, Bureau of Vital Statistics, NJ. On this birth certificate, the surname of the mother is listed as "Edith Mae Spjut." This is an unusual surname, but the letter "j" is quite deliberate. See also the birth certificates for her children. [RP018]

[337]Birth Certificate of Bonnie Jean Komarek; Birth No. 129-57-116069; Reg. No. 1623; NJ Dept. of Health and Senior Services. [RP018]

[338]Marriage Record of John F. Hall and Bonnie Jean Komarek, No. 91 7536 (92 012938) recorded in Pinellas Co., FL; Book 235, p. 533 (07 Jan. 1992). [RP018]

[339]Information regarding the birth of Ryan Samuel Hall was supplied to the author by his grandfather, Robert Edwin

Komarek. Efforts to verify these data have been unsuccessful. The Illinois Department of Phblic Health, Division of Vital Records considers this information to be confidential, as detailed in their correspondence to the author dated 24 June 1997. [RP018]

[340]Birth Certificate of Robert John Komarek; Birth No. 129-62318; Reg. No. 928; NJ Dept. of Health and Senior Services. [RP018]

[341]Information regarding the marriage between Robert John Komarek and Maria Falcon was supplied to the author by the groom's father, Robert Edwin Komarek. Efforts to verify these data have been unsuccessful. The *Departamento de Salud Registro Demografico*, P. O. Box 11854, San Juan, Puerto Rico 00910 considers this information to be confidential, as detailed in their correspondence to the author dated 23 June 1997 and 22 July 1997. [RP018]

[342]Birth Certificate of William Franklin Frotscher, Jr., State Dept. of Health, Bureau of Vital Statistics, NJ. [RP008]

[343]Marriage Certificate No. 172271 of William Franklin Frotscher, Jr. and Cherry A. Cooper dated 01 August 1959, at Chester, Delaware Co., PA. [RP008]

[344]Birth Certificate of Cherry Aurelia Winford, No. 42542; filed 21 Feb. 1936 from St. Paul, Ramsey Co., MN; the surname, "Cooper," is from her stepfather, Clarence Cooper. [RP008]

[345]Marriage License of William Franklin Frotscher and Sarah Anne Buttermore dated 26 June 1997; copy provided by Mary C. Lewis, Clerk of Orphans' Court, Cumberland Co., PA. [RP008]

[346]Confirmation of birth record from Georgia Department of Human Resources, Atlanta, GA in letter dated 27 June 1997, to the author. [RP008]

[347]Marriage Record of Franklin Co., PA, Vol. 89, p. 335. [RP012]

[348]*Ibid.*

[349]Birth Announcement reported the *News Chronicle*, Shippensburg, PA; 19 June 1997. [RP012]

[350]Death Certificate of William Franklin Frotscher-III, Pennsylvania Division of Vital Records, New Castle, PA 16103-1528. [RP008]

[351]Death Certificate of Jennifer L. Frotscher, Pennsylvania Division of Vital Records, New Castle, PA 16103-1528. [RP008]

[352][Shippensburg, PA] *News Chronicle* - 02 Aug. 1995.

[353]Birth announcements, *News Chronicle* - 16 Jan. 1997.

[354]Birth Certificate of Earl Franklin Skelton, issued by the Hackensack Hospital; New Jersey Certificate and Record of Birth, issued 26 April 1940 and Birth Certificate of Earl Franklin Skelton, State Dept. of Health, Bureau of Vital Statistics, NJ. `[RP026]

[355]Certificate of Marriage, dated 13 July 1962 issued by the New Jersey State Department of Health. [RP026]

[356]Certificate of Birth Registration of Anita Patton, No. 22884, issued by the City of New York, NY. [RP026]

[357]Superior Court of the District of Columbia, Family Division, Domestic Relations Branch, Civil Action No. D1105-84; Anita P. Skelton, Plaintiff, vs. Earl F. Skelton, Defendant. [RP026]

[358]Certificate of Marriage, dated 19 October 1986, License No. 121570 issued by the Clerk of the Superior Court of the District of Columbia. [RP026]

[359]Certificate of Birth of Thelma Francine Fried; Certificate No. 29615, issued by the Department of Health, Borough of Manhattan, City of New York, NY. Known throughout much of her life as "Thelma," in her later years she chose to be called "Francesca," a variant of her middle name. [RP026]

[360]Certificate of Birth for Diane Lynne Skelton issued by the Samarital Hospital, Troy, NY; Certificate of Birth Registration, NY State Dept. of Health,

Office of Vital Records, filed 27 Sep. 1965; Certificate of Birth No. 129545. [RP026]

361The second marriage, although performed by a rabbi, was not officially recorded. In a letter to the author dated 17 October 1997, Vera I. Stanley, Marriage Clerk of the Superior Court of the District of Columbia, stated that there was no record of a marriage between Patrice Yves Faujour and Diana Lynne Skelton in the year 1989. [RP026]

362Certificate of Marriage, dated 24 Jun. 1989; "EXTRAIT DE L'ACTE DE MARIAGE N° 4" issued by the Mayor of Cox, France. (A copy is in the possession of the author.) [RP026]

363Birth Registration Certificate for Joline Mariya Faujour, MD State Dept. of Health and Mental Hygiene, Division of Vital Records, filed 07 Feb. 1991; State File No. 91-04134. [RP026]

364Birth Registration Certificate for Délora Kathline Faujour, No. 002706, filed by the Mayor of Melun, France on 08 Dec. 1993. Also, a Consular Report of Birth [of a U.S. Citizen] Abroad was filed on 26 Jan. 1994 at the U.S. Embassy in Paris, France. [RP026]

365The paternal ancestors of this Skelton family have been traced by the author through four generations: (1) Isaac Franklin (b. 22 Sep. 1861, IceCreek, OH - d. 31 Oct. 1932, Dayton, KY); (2) Isaac (b. Oct. 1822, Scioto Co., OH - d. 11 Jan. 1896, Ironton, OH); (3) Samuel (b. 1783, Shenandoah Co., VA - d. Mar. 1857, Scioto Co., OH); and (4) John (b. ca. 1750 - d. 1816/1817, Shenandoah Co., VA).

366The paternal ancestors of this Patton family have been traced by the author through six generations: (1) Kenneth Grayson (b. 03 Jul. 1915, Chicago, IL - d. 18 Jul. 1987, Columbus, OH); (2) Felix Grayson (b. 11 Oct. 1869, Ritchie Co., WV - d. — ? —); (3) John Sutton (b. 13 Jul. 1841, Quincy, OH - d. 28 Dec. 1919, Leavenworth, KS); (4)

Benjamin (b. 1812, Harrison Co., VA - d. — ? —); (5) John (b. ca. 1775, in Harrison Co., VA - d. 21 Apr. 1837); and (6) Francis (b. ca. 1742 - d. ca. 1797, in Harrison Co., VA).

367Birth Certificate for Isaac Patton Skelton issued by the Department of Human Services, District of Columbia, No. 108-71-022247; recorded 18 Nov. 1971. [RP026]

368Certificate of Marriage Registration of Isaac Patton Skelton and Dana Sevastyanova from the City of New York, Office of the City Clerk, Marriage License Bureau, No. M96214034; License No. M96025321

369Certificate of Naturalization of Dana Segal Skelton, No. 22501671 (INS Reg. No. A70 326 826).

370Birth Certificate of Dora Segal Skelton, New York State Dept. of Health, Register No. 1294, filed 30 Sep. 1997.

www.ingramcontent.com/pod-product-compliance
Lightning Source LLC
Chambersburg PA
CBHW050223270326
41914CB00003BA/541